FRIDGE RAID

MEGAN DAVIES

FRIDGE
RAID

**FLEXIBLE, KITCHEN-FORAGED
RECIPES FOR LOW-WASTE MEALS**

PHOTOGRAPHY BY RITA PLATTS

RYLAND PETERS & SMALL
LONDON • NEW YORK

DEDICATION
To the wriggling sproglet in my tummy, who has also been a taste tester for the entire book without even knowing!

Senior Designer Megan Smith
Senior Editor Gillian Haslam
Head of Production Patricia Harrington
Art Director Leslie Harrington
Editorial Director Julia Charles
Publisher Cindy Richards

Food Stylist Megan Davies
Food Stylist's Assistant Sarah Vassallo
Prop Stylist Hannah Wilkinson
Indexer Hilary Bird
Cover Illustrator Bryony Clarkson

Published in 2021
by Ryland Peters & Small
20–21 Jockey's Fields
London WC1R 4BW
and
341 E 116th St
New York NY 10029
www.rylandpeters.com

Text © Megan Davies 2021
Design and photographs
© Ryland Peters & Small 2021
Cover illustration © Bryony Clarkson 2021

MIX
Paper from
responsible sources
FSC® C106563

ISBN: 978-1-78879-361-2

10 9 8 7 6 5 4 3 2 1

Printed and bound in China.

CIP data from the Library of Congress has been applied for. A CIP record for this book is available from the British Library.

NOTES
* Both British (metric) and American (imperial plus US cup) measurements are included in these recipes; however, it is important to work with one set of measurements and not alternate between the two within a recipe.
* All butter is salted unless specified.
* All eggs are medium (UK) or large (US), unless specified as large, in which case US extra-large should be used. Uncooked or partially cooked eggs should not be served to the very old, frail, young children, pregnant women or those with compromised immune systems.
* Ovens should be preheated to the specified temperatures. We recommend using an oven thermometer.
* When a recipe calls for the grated zest of citrus fruit, buy unwaxed fruit and wash well before using. If you can only find treated fruit, scrub well in warm soapy water before using.

CONTENTS

INTRODUCTION

Fridge Raid is an honest, practical and, I hope, very useful cookbook. There aren't lists of fancy ingredients or 10-hour recipes scattered across the pages; instead you will find a collection of humble, flexible, simple recipes, the majority of which were originally genuine 'fridge-foraged' meals that I came up with on the spot in my kitchen here in London.

The moment I thought of gathering together all these ideas into a book, I started writing down my recipes, continuing to do so throughout the four seasons and found I had gathered almost a book's worth of content! These recipes were conjured up using nothing but a notebook and what I had in the fridge, freezer, cupboard, vegetable rack or fruit bowl. Of course, I then fine-tuned the list and topped up with some new dishes to round things off, but the majority of this book really is a compilation of naturally developed 'fridge raid' meals.

As I hadn't yet shared my book idea with my publisher, this process of 'invention without pressure' not only allowed me to create recipes freely, but it also made me reflect on the way we run our kitchens. Rummaging around to see which limp herbs I needed to use up or which canned beans I might find in the cupboard made me really acknowledge the food and produce we have access to, and, in such a disposable culture, how important it is to cherish each ingredient. How? Simply by using those ingredients in the most efficient and sustainable way, stretching, utilizing, being inventive and flexible! I don't mean fermenting or pickling everything in sight – I just mean respecting what we've spent our hard-earned cash on and making it stretch as far as possible. It's also very similar to how our grandparents (and their parents) used to run their kitchens. This is what *Fridge Raid* is all about.

I have divided the book into six main sections, the majority of which are dictated by the seasons, reflecting the produce that is at its best and the things I particularly crave at those times of year. So you'll find warming stews and slow-cook meals in the winter chapter, barbecue recipes and bold salads in the summer chapter, and so on. I have also tried always to include store-cupboard items in every recipe, so that if you can't get hold of the fresh ingredients that I suggest, you can use what you've got.

One of the other recipe chapters that opens the book is Everyday Staples where I've laid out some basic ingredients you are quite likely to have at home, and based recipes around those hero ingredients. We've got eggs, cheese, milk and yogurt, bread, then pastry and potatoes. Some of them are very basic, and some of them involve more preparation, but all of them are focused on the 'staple' ingredient. Also at the front of the book is the Kitchen Condiments chapter, where you'll find dips, sauces, dressings, spreads and chutneys that can liven up any sandwich, loaded toast, simple supper or boring salad. They're very straight forward, too. It can be exhausting to feel as though you have to jazz up every meal of the week (there's also not enough time) but what you can do is make a batch of condiments one slow Sunday, leave them in the fridge and know that when you grab a quick bagel, bowl of soup or eggs on toast, you've got a great additional dip or sauce to freshen things up (and possibly clear out the salad drawer).

So, that's all the chapters explained, which leads me on to telling you about the ingredients tables that I've conjured up for you. In my last book, I included a couple of notes at the bottom of every single recipe sharing brief 'swap-in' and 'leftovers' ideas, in order to help inspire you to use what you've got and to stretch your food.

My ingredients tables are basically a deep dive into this concept and the aim is to encourage you to develop an intuition when it comes to swapping alternative ingredients for the original ones I started with.

On every recipe you'll see a simple, two-column table. The left-hand side shows the original ingredients I created the recipe with, which you are more than welcome to abide by; however I actually encourage you to use that as a (close) guide, but then refer to the right-hand column and see the alternative suggestions for other ingredients that would work well, too. This will help you save money, shopping time, energy in all its guises and make use of your existing stock! I have tried to add several alternative ideas for

every ingredient, but there's no need to stick even to those, if you have another that you think could work, try it! You can't go too far wrong, I promise. I've also added tips alongside each recipe, to suggest what goes well with each dish and inspiration for what to do with any leftovers.

Finally, on the following pages I've added a few notes on seasoning, oils, food prep, storage and so on. It's simple, confidence-boosting advice on getting the most out of the food you've bought and running your kitchen more sustainably.

So, go raid the fridge and cupboards, see what you've got and find a recipe in here that suits. I really hope you enjoy using this book and gain more than just a lovely meal or two out of it. Happy sustainable cooking and even happier raiding!

USEFUL COOKING TIPS

Here I've shared a handful of simple cooking tips and advice that will not only aid you in using this book with ease, but also generally in the kitchen. Having a base knowledge of oils, seasoning and nuggets of prepping information will really help confidence and flow when cooking. So, have a read through and refer back if you're ever stuck.

SEASONING INGREDIENTS

+ I always use sea salt flakes for seasoning during and after cooking.

+ When seasoning water for pasta, grains or veg, I use cheaper, fine sea salt crystals (table salt is also ok).

+ You can use mixed peppercorns, or white pepper, but my go-to (like most people) is freshly cracked black pepper.

+ Try out ingredients instead of salt: soy sauce or tamari (gluten-free soy), Marmite/yeast extract, Bovril or hard cheeses, like Parmesan. Also, olives, capers and anchovies are staples in my kitchen and often get thrown in as an alternative salty hit with more depth.

SEASONING TIPS AND NOTES ON BALANCE

+ Season throughout the cooking process – I'll often prompt you to do this in my recipes. Don't forget the most important thing about seasoning, though, is to taste! Taste, season, taste and season again. In my opinion, people often under-season, which is just a confidence thing, so don't be shy! We are often told how bad for us salt and butter are, but I say just get it in there.

+ If you think something is too salty, give it a dash of sweetness to even things out (honey or any sugar for example).

+ Likewise, try a squeeze of lemon or lime juice, which lifts and cuts through a dish. Fragrant herbs also help with this; parsley or mint, say.

+ If something is too sweet, use the tip above but the other way around – add something salty (or spicy for that matter)!

+ If something is too spicy, add a mellowing ingredient (either folded in or served alongside); dairy is your best friend here: milk, yogurt, cheese, cream, crème fraîche etc.

+ If something tastes sour, or too tart, add sweetness.

+ Making a salad dressing is a great way to train your taste buds and put your intuition to the test – more mustard, more honey, more vinegar, some lemon. See how you get on!

OILS AND FATS – WHAT TO USE AND WHEN

+ Rapeseed/canola/veg/sunflower oil: These are the oils with a high burning point (least likely to burn your food at high temperatures), but generally with a much milder (or no) flavour. Use these when you want to get things nice and crisp (high-heat frying, hot and quick or deep frying). Rapeseed/canola is my favourite and the best for you (most labelled veg oils in the UK are pure rapeseed oil).

+ Olive oil: My most used 'cooking oil', I use olive oil for so many things, including medium-heat frying and roasting. You can't go too far wrong with olive oil – it has a lovely flavour and is very versatile.

+ Extra virgin olive oil: Don't cook with it – it's the most expensive and luxurious! Save it for salad dressings, no-cook sauces, drizzling and finishing dishes with. If you save it for these times, then you can use it liberally with joy!

+ Butter and ghee (clarified butter): You can use it whenever you might use olive oil, so for low- to medium-heat frying/pan cooking. Note that butter will burn quicker, so watch out. Anything cooked in butter is always going to be dreamy and I love using it. It can be used in a pan and in the oven. Add it to veg or grains, as you would when roasting a chicken, it's lush.

+ Sesame or nut oils: For flavouring salad dressings or drizzling on finished dishes, like extra virgin olive oil. However, I often use sesame oil (mixed with rapeseed/canola oil) for medium-high frying, such as in the Tofu Noodles with Mushrooms and Marmite (page 77).

+ Coconut oil: I have to say I'm not a fan, unless there is coconut present in the actual recipe (like my Yellow Fish Curry, page 81), then I would happily use it. To me it's over-powering when used in Western dishes so I avoid it. But, if you like it, by all means use it.

PREPPING VEG AND HERBS

+ I tend not to peel anything, so unless I specify, don't either. It's a waste, there's plenty of goodness in the skin or peel of produce and all skin really needs is a good rinse in cold water to get rid of any soil or pesticides. Skins (when fried or roasted) also add a lovely texture and bite, so it's also enjoyable!

+ The same goes for herb stalks – if they're soft, use them all. Freeze or chuck hard stems into water

jugs/pitchers. If you don't like the idea of whole stalks with your leafy herb garnish, thinly slice the stalks and add them to the pan with your onion/veg.

+ A couple of notes on ginger: I don't peel it. The skin has a really great kick and whilst it may feel weird, you won't notice once it's been cooked. It adds a welcome warmth to your dish, and no peeling means less waste and effort. Also, I find grating ginger is a faff and you lose lots of it (both juice and flesh) in the process, so I cut it into thin matchsticks.

SPICES

+ As you can imagine, I'm not fussy about whole or ground spices. Of course, it's great for authenticity to use what's asked for, but I'm more about using what you've got. So if a recipe suggests one but you have the other – use it!

+ Obviously whole spices are better for texture, and if you crush them they release lovely oils and fragrance, but there's no need to buy them if you have a perfectly good ground version already in the cupboard.

SUBSTITUTIONS AND SWAPPING IN

+ I won't write much about this here because I have shared lots of ideas in every single recipe as you'll see. The main point is to use what you've got, I really mean this.

+ As you start to cook in this way, you will begin to develop an idea about what works well, what you like (and don't). It's all about confidence. Use the table and the options I've suggested to get you going and see where you end up.

+ The beauty of savoury cooking (and most of this book's recipes are, for that exact reason) is that you can change stuff up a bit and the recipe will still work pretty well.

+ Obviously baking and sweet foods are more 'restricted' in terms of playing with their ingredients and quantities, so that's why I've not focused too much on puddings and sweets.

STERILIZING JARS FOR FOOD STORAGE

+ Storing chutneys, pickles or any homemade, long-life food needs to be done using a freshly sterilized jar. It sounds annoying, but it's so easy – there are two options:

+ Run it through your dishwasher, job done. Or...

+ Preheat the oven to 150°C fan/170°C/325°F/ Gas 3, wash the jars and lids with warm soapy water, rinse, then place the clean (but still wet) jars upside down on a baking sheet. Transfer to the oven and 'sterilize' in there for 15 minutes. Let them cool, then fill with whatever you want.

+ If your jars have removable rubber seals, wash these by hand.

STORING THINGS IN THE FRIDGE

+ Treat yourself to some good-quality sealable containers, or like me, hoard plastic takeaway/take-out containers and allocate a proper home for them in the kitchen so you always have something to pop leftovers in. If that part is easy, you're less likely to find it a faff saving, stretching and repurposing your food.

+ I have to say, whilst 'food safety' is very important, you can also just pop an upside-down plate on top of a bowl to avoid food drying out in the fridge.

+ One other very beneficial practice is keeping your fridge organized. Have separate and constant areas (or shelves, depending on fridge size) for dairy, meat, veg, salads, herbs, root veg and condiments. It sounds simple, but again, you will benefit from this!

+ Label every item you freeze. You're way more likely to actually use those frozen breadcrumbs, leftover caramel sauce tubs, stock trimmings and frozen ragù if you actually know what they are when you find them six months later.

WASTE

+ Don't throw out food with the rest of your household trash! If you have food waste to get rid of, please compost it.

+ If you don't already have a food and garden waste bin at home, your council may be able to provide you with one. If you have the space, create your own compost pile at the bottom of the garden and use it!

+ When you are cooking, grab a couple of bowls for waste. Use one for normal waste (unrecyclable packaging) and the other for food waste, and if you have any recyclable packaging,

throw it in the sink so it gets cleaned and put in the recycling. This sounds really basic but it's so easy not to bother when you're in a rush or tired. It's all about habit, so be strict for a couple of weeks and you'll end up doing so without thinking.

+ Then, when you're done, go through that food waste bowl and freeze what might be able to be saved. The two main groups I would focus on are trimmings and bones for stock, then fruit peel and trimmings for drinks!

+ Obviously, keep any raw meat separate to the veg or fruit you might re-purpose, so keep an eye on that.

+ I have three big freezer bags always on the go that I add to as and when. One is for bones (raw and cooked), another for all the veg and herb trimmings and peelings (think root veg, onion skins, carrot tops, leeks, herb trimmings or hardy stalks, celeriac/celery root, swede/rutabaga, spring onions/scallions, cabbage etc) for making stocks, and one that I add fruit peelings and trimmings to, which I add to water jugs/pitchers in the summer for flavour, without spending money on fresh fruit, but to the same effect (and it's frozen so acts like ice!).

+ If it's a fruit that goes brown once cut, such as apple wedges, just squeeze some lemon or lime juice over it to avoid this.

+ I always freeze blackened bananas separately. They are incredible for baking when black, frozen and de-frosted. Amazingly sweet and so soft they're almost runny.

+ Start doing all of the above and you will have an abundant stock pan before you know it, bountiful jugs of fruity water and have made all that produce double, if not triple, in its use.

EVERYDAY
STAPLES

EGGS
EGGS & CHEESE ON TOAST

I'm killing two birds with one stone here. I love eggs on toast and I love on cheese on toast. This is a combo of the two, with an encased runny egg in the centre and a rich, bubbling cheese mix on top. It's really simple and is a great pimped-up, yet simple lunch. Use whatever cheese, chutney or mustard you have, and the same goes for bread. The only thing you really do need is an egg.

2 large slices of sourdough bread	Use any bread. If frozen, defrost in the toaster
2 eggs	Essential, but any size can be used
180 g/6½ oz. mature Cheddar	Any cheese – hard is best, but you can use soft if it's all you have
20 g/4 teaspoons Dijon mustard	Wholegrain or English, or even mustard powder (in which case, halve the amount)
40 g/2 tablespoons mango chutney	Any chutney, or a mix of several
Worcestershire sauce	A little apple cider or balsamic vinegar
sea salt and freshly ground pepper	
SERVES 2	*TOTAL TIME 15 MINUTES*

Preheat the oven to 250°C fan/270°C/500°F/Gas 10, or as hot as your oven will go.

Toast the bread (either in the toaster, or both sides under the grill/broiler), then place the slices in a single layer on a large baking sheet. Using your fist, press down firmly on the centre of each piece of toast, to make a wide well for the egg.

Grate the cheese into a bowl, then add the mustard, chutney, a few shakes of Worcestershire sauce and a pinch of seasoning. Mix well to combine.

Crack an egg into each of the toast wells, then place the baking sheet in the preheated oven on the highest shelf for 4 minutes. Remove from the oven and top each toast with the cheese mixture. Return to the oven and bake for another 4 minutes until the eggs are set with a runny yolk and the cheese is melted, bubbly and golden.

Remove from the oven, let sit for 30 seconds, then eat immediately.

GOES WELL WITH Brown Sauce (page 63).

LEFTOVERS Unlikely to be any!

BAKED EGGS

Baked eggs are the perfect Sunday night supper, when you've had a big lunch and just want something comforting but simple to eat in front of the TV. The fillings can be determined by what you have in the fridge. It might be leftover roast items, a curry, stir-fried greens, a chilli/chile... there are so many options (see below for inspiration). I add the fillings and then the egg, adding lighter things like cheese, cream or herbs on top, but have a go and see which way you like best.

2 teaspoons butter, at room temperature	Any oil
4–5 tablespoons filling per egg: see across for some ideas	Leftover roasted veg, ragù, cooked meat, baked beans, meaty curry, dahl, soup, stir fry, pasta sauce (any kind), fresh leafy greens, sliced raw tomatoes, smoked salmon, sliced mushrooms, fresh soft herbs, fresh spinach, cooked potato slices, chips/fries, cheese, leftover fry-up or Sunday roast items, ricotta, stew, tagine... the list goes on!
4 eggs	Essential, but any size can be used
4 tablespoons single/light cream	Not essential, but I like a slosh of cream in baked eggs
sea salt and freshly ground pepper	
toast, to serve	
SERVES 4	**TOTAL TIME 15–20 MINUTES**

4 ramekins or a couple of shallow ovenproof dishes, depending whether you want individual baked eggs or a sharing set-up

Preheat the oven to 230°C fan/250°C/475°F/Gas 9.

Grease the ramekins or dishes with the butter, then fill with your chosen fillings. Break an egg into each ramekin (or 2 eggs per dish) over the top of the fillings, then pour over a splash of cream and a sprinkle of seasoning.

Place the ramekins or dishes on a baking sheet and bake in the preheated oven for 10–14 minutes until cooked through but softly set. If it's a thicker ramekin or you've chosen a larger dish with multiple eggs inside, the eggs may need a little longer in the oven (this is because cold fillings in the ramekins absorb some of that heat, so after 10 minutes, keep a close eye on them but remember that they'll continue to cook slightly once out the oven). Serve with toast.

GOES WELL WITH Hunk of Cheese Scones (page 26), breadcrumbs (page 37) and the Mixed Bean Salad (page 91).

LEFTOVERS Scooped out of their ramekins and piled into pitta breads as egg and 'something' sandwiches. Add some mustard and mayo and they'll be lovely!

EGGY BREAD WITH PEAS & CAPERS

As a child I used to love eating eggy bread with ketchup (a combination I still love!). This, however, is a more grown-up savoury version, but you still get a natural sweetness from the peas. I tend to use defrosted sliced bread (one of my freezer staples), but it works really well with any bread you have in the freezer. Or even better, fresh bread!

2 eggs	Essential, but any size can be used
30 ml/2 tablespoons whole milk	Any type of milk, dairy-free too
30 g/2 tablespoons unsalted butter	Any butter, or use a flavourless oil
4 slices of bread	Any bread. If frozen, de-frosted
20 g/2 tablespoons capers, drained	Roughly chopped olives or cornichons
100 g/¾ cup frozen peas	Fresh peas, or frozen edamame, sweetcorn/corn kernels or green beans
sea salt and freshly ground pepper	
SERVES 2	*TOTAL TIME 20 MINUTES*

Preheat the oven to 100°C fan/120°C/250°F/Gas ½. Place an ovenproof plate on the bottom shelf of the oven.

Whisk the eggs and milk in a shallow bowl with a generous pinch of seasoning. Heat half the butter in a non-stick frying pan/skillet over a medium heat.

Add a slice of bread to the egg bowl and slosh it around so it absorbs some of the egg mixture, then flip it over and slosh around once more.

Once the butter has melted and is gently sizzling in the pan, transfer the eggy bread to the pan and fry for about 3 minutes on each side, until both sides are golden brown and crispy-edged. While the first slice is cooking, place a second piece of bread in the egg bowl to soak.

When the first slice of bread is done, transfer it to the warming plate in the oven and cook the next slice in the same way. Repeat the process until all 4 slices have been cooked. Use the remaining butter as needed.

When the pan is empty, pop the capers and peas straight in, with a small splash of water and twist of pepper. Fry for about 3 minutes, until they're tender and starting to catch a little. As they cook, gently mash them in the pan with the back of a fork. Taste to check for seasoning.

Halve the eggy bread, divide between serving plates, then pile the peas and capers on top and serve immediately.

GOES WELL WITH Brown Sauce (page 63).

LEFTOVERS Chop the bread up a bit and fry it all together in a large pan. Serve with fresh tomatoes and salad, like crunchy, eggy croutons and greens!

RISOTTO FRITTATA

Frittatas are the ultimate 'chuck-it-in' and 'use-it-up' recipe. Here I have used leftover Dried Mushroom Risotto (page 133). The creamy, saucy risotto rice goes crispy and chewy where it catches at the pan edges whilst the rest, encased in the egg mixture, remains soft and satisfying. Try adding other extras too, such as chopped-up bacon and more greens or herbs. Take care with the seasoning if adding lots of salty things as you've already got a (hopefully) well-seasoned risotto in there.

1 red onion	Any onion or shallot, spring onion/scallion or celery
250 g/2 cups leftover Dried Mushroom Risotto (page 133)	Leftover paella, fried-rice dish, steamed rice
6 eggs	Essential
30 ml/2 tablespoons milk	Any milk you like, single/light cream or sour cream
150 g/1 cup frozen peas	Fresh peas, spring onion/scallion, spinach, soft herbs
150 g/5½ oz. mozzarella	Goat's cheese, Brie, cream cheese, Emmental
olive oil, for cooking	
sea salt and freshly ground pepper	
SERVES 4	**TOTAL TIME 30 MINUTES**

24-cm/9½-inch non-stick, oven-safe frying pan/skillet

Halve, peel and thinly slice the onion. Add a drizzle of oil to the frying pan/skillet and set over a medium heat. When the oil is hot, add the onion and fry for 5 minutes until softening. Next, add the risotto to the pan and roughly break it up with a wooden spoon, making sure the heat can penetrate through all the rice. Let the onion and risotto mixture fry for another 5 minutes, stirring often.

In a jug/pitcher, whisk the eggs and milk with a fork, then season. Add the peas to the pan, let them defrost for a couple of minutes, then reduce the heat to low-medium. Add the egg mixture to the pan, quickly distribute the fillings evenly within the egg and then leave to set on the hob/stovetop for about 7 minutes – don't stir!

Meanwhile, preheat the grill/broiler to high.

Once the frittata is almost set but with the egg still runny in the centre, tear the mozzarella and scatter over the top. Set the pan under the preheated grill/broiler and let finish cooking for 3–5 minutes, until just set and the mozzarella is lightly golden.

Let the frittata rest for a couple of minutes, then transfer to a board and slice to serve.

GOES WELL WITH It's really nice with either the Apple and Cumin Slaw (page 162) or the Celery Waldorf (page 182).

LEFTOVERS Best as is, or just re-heat in a very hot oven until piping hot (this is very important as leftover rice must be thoroughly reheated).

CHEESE
CHEESEBOARD PASTIES WITH ONION & HERBS

Who doesn't love melting cheese and pastry together? This is a riff on the classic cheese and onion pasty/bake, but with a mix of whatever cheese you have that needs using up. A general rule of thumb is if it's hard cheese, coarsely grate it and if it's soft, tear into chunks. If it's really soft, like ricotta, spoon in at the last moment and don't over-fold. Try not to overload with super-strong cheeses, like blue cheese, but otherwise anything goes. These pasties are great for supper time with a salad on the side, picnics, car lunches, and so many other situations. They're really versatile and I love them all year round, I hope you do too.

1 egg	A splash of whole milk (or any type)
1 onion	Spring onion/scallion, shallot, celery, fennel
2 spring onions/scallions	Shallot, red or white onion, celery, fennel
30 g/2 tablespoons butter	Olive oil, rapeseed/canola oil or sunflower oil
2 garlic cloves	Chopped/lazy garlic or purée
60 g/2½ oz. hard cheese	Cheddar, Manchego, Parmesan, Wensleydale, Pecorino, Gorgonzola, Emmental
60 g/2½ oz. soft cheese	Goat's, soft blue, cream, feta, ricotta, mozzarella
6 sprigs of fresh thyme	Fresh oregano or chives are nice
1 sheet of ready-made puff pastry, 320 g/11½ oz.	Best to use puff pastry here, or make some homemade rough puff pastry
6 tablespoons chutney	Any chutney – I love mango, fig, onion, or good old Branston Pickle
½ teaspoon nigella seeds	Sesame seeds (black or white), cumin seeds or chilli/hot red pepper flakes (use less of these)
celery stick/stalks, to serve	Wedges of Gem/Boston lettuce or any salad you like
English mustard, to serve	Whatever condiments you like!
sea salt and freshly ground pepper	
SERVES 6 AS A SNACK, OR 3 AS A MEAL	*TOTAL TIME 70 MINUTES, PLUS CHILLING*

Line a large baking sheet with parchment paper.

Break the egg into a mug, season and briefly whisk with a fork, then set aside.

Halve, peel and finely slice the onion and spring onions/scallions. Melt the butter in a large, non-stick frying pan/skillet over a medium heat. Once the butter is sizzling, add the onions and gently fry for 20 minutes until caramelized, stirring very often to avoid burning. Peel and thinly slice the garlic cloves. When the onions are golden and soft, add the garlic and fry for another minute or two, then remove from the heat and let cool to room temperature.

Grate the hard cheese into a large mixing bowl, then tear the soft cheese into 5-cm/2-inch chunks and add that too. Pinch the top of a thyme stalks and scrape down to the end, releasing the tiny leaves, then add these to the cheese.

Unroll the sheet of puff pastry and cut into 6 equal squares. Spread a tablespoon of the chutney onto each square, leaving a 1-cm/½-inch clear border around each square.

Transfer the cooled onions to the cheese bowl and fold the ingredients together. Taste to check for seasoning and then divide the mixture into the centre of each pastry square, on top of the chutney.

Brush all around the clear border of one pastry square with the egg wash and then bring two opposite corners together over the centre of the mixture. Press the edges together to seal and, if you wish, use your fingers to create a chunky crimp.

Brush the sealed pasty with more egg wash and transfer to the prepared baking sheet. Repeat the sealing process for the remaining pasties. Sprinkle over the nigella seeds and transfer to the fridge to firm up for 30 minutes (or overnight if you're making ahead, just loosely cover them with a tea/dish towel if so).

Preheat the oven to 200°C fan/220°C/425°F/Gas 7.

Place the baking sheet on the top shelf of the preheated oven and bake for 30 minutes until golden brown. Remove from the oven, let sit for a couple of minutes, then serve with celery sticks/stalks and English mustard.

GOES WELL WITH A brew (of tea or coffee) or a beer.

LEFTOVERS Just heat up and have as they are.

HUNK OF CHEESE SCONES

These scones are not only moreish, but perfect for using up odd corners or hunks of cheese. I often make them with a mix of cheeses, but they are also lovely with just one kind. The most important thing for a successful bake is to use a strong, hard cheese (see suggestions below). Heavy soft cheeses seem to weigh down the mix and anything mild gets a bit lost.

220 g/1⅔ cups self-raising/rising flour	Wholemeal/whole-wheat self-raising/rising, or plain/all-purpose flour + 2 teaspoons baking powder
½ teaspoon sea salt	¼ teaspoon table salt
1 teaspoon mustard powder	Omit, or use a pinch of cayenne pepper
50 g/3½ tablespoons cold butter	Ideally use butter, but can substitute margarine
100 g/3½ oz. hard cheese	Mature Cheddar, Parmesan or a sturdy blue cheese
80 ml/5½ tablespoons whole milk, plus extra for brushing	Any sort of milk
30 ml/2 tablespoons water	
MAKES 6	*TOTAL TIME 35 MINUTES*

6-cm/2½-inch cookie cutter, pastry brush, baking sheet lined with parchment paper

Preheat the oven to 220°C fan/240°C/475°F/Gas 9.

Add the flour, salt and mustard powder to a large mixing bowl, then run your fingers through it to mix up. Chop the butter into small cubes, add to the bowl and rub into the flour mix to make sandy breadcrumbs. I find grabbing a handful and rubbing my fingers against my thumbs whilst I lift my hands up, letting the rubbed mix fall down into the bowl, works well, and it stops the butter getting too warm in your hands.

Grate almost all the cheese into the bowl (save a small handful for the tops of the scones) and fold it through the flour mixture. Make a well in the centre and pour in the milk and water. Using a metal spoon, bring the dough together until the liquid has been incorporated. You don't want to overwork the dough, so be brief. Tip the mixture onto a lightly floured surface. Press the dough down to a thickness of about 3 cm/1¼ inches (again, don't overwork it, so don't use a rolling pin). Press your cookie cutter into the dough and cut out some scones. Pop these on the lined baking sheet, then bring the remaining dough together, push it down slightly and cut out more scones until all the dough has been used. You should get about 6 scones.

Brush a little milk over the tops of the scones, then grate the remaining cheese over. Place on the top shelf of the preheated oven and bake for 12–14 minutes until light golden brown on top. Watch them, as they don't need long! Let them cool for 5 minutes, then serve.

GOES WELL WITH Butter and Marmite/yeast extract, Date and Nut Chutney (page 62), ham, more cheese... They're also lovely on their own, straight out of the oven and still warm.

LEFTOVERS They freeze really well. Heat from frozen until warm and defrosted.

MARINATED FETA

This is possibly the quickest, simplest and most delicious thing you could spend 5 minutes doing. You won't ever want to have feta straight from a packet or pot once you've tried this, I promise. The beauty of it, too, is that you can pretty much marinate the cheese with whatever you choose – I like the ingredients below, but play around with different whole spices, fresh herbs and chillies/chiles. You can also add sun-dried/sun-blush tomatoes, olives, anchovies or artichokes, to name a few additions. If you do add these though, make sure you consume within a few days.

200 g/1½ cups good-quality feta cheese	Essential
1 fresh red chilli/chile, halved lengthways	Any chilli/chile is great here, fresh, dried, any colour, or chilli/hot red pepper flakes
3 small dried chillies/chiles	As above, use what you've got or leave out
½ teaspoon fennel seeds	Cumin, coriander or caraway seeds
8 black peppercorns	Pink or mixed peppercorns
1 bay leaf	Fresh or dried, or leave out if you don't have any
6 garlic cloves, peeled	If you're out of garlic, lemon peel is great
2 fresh dill stalks, left whole	Any fresh herbs, such as parsley or basil
300–400 ml/1¼–1⅔ cups good-quality extra virgin olive oil	Olive oil or cold-pressed rapeseed/canola oil
SERVES 4–6	**TOTAL TIME 5 MINUTES**

Sterilized jam jars (see page 10 for how to sterilize) of any size, or any sealable container

Break up the feta into large chunks, then add to the sterilized jar(s) with all the 'flavourings'. Fill the jars with the olive oil, or until the ingredients are all submerged.

Store in the fridge, but remove from the fridge for at least 30 minutes before use so the olive oil can loosen up (it'll harden in the cold).

GOES WELL WITH Marinated feta is incredibly versatile. Try it on toast, with the Chorizo and Butter Bean Chilli (page 71), as a filling for the Wonky Stuffed Flatbreads (page 42), with the Mixed Bean Salad (page 91), with the Cayenne-roasted Sprouts (page 178), the list really does go on.

LEFTOVERS You don't need to do anything to the leftovers, treat it as a condiment and once the feta and chilli have been eaten, use the oil for marinades, cooking or dressings. Just avoid using it for recipes where you wouldn't want any faint hints of cheese.

YOGURT & MILK
BACK-OF-THE-SPICE-CUPBOARD MARINADE

Now, this 'recipe' may seem very unhelpful at first glance, but in fact the reason it is so vague is because you can literally use whatever ingredients you would like to use up. Of course, there are combinations that work particularly well together, so here I've included four different lists of combinations that I would happily use.

200 ml/¾ cup whole milk	Any milk, dairy-free milk, coconut milk, yogurt
dried spices and herbs	See below for plenty of ideas
MAKES A BATCH TO COAT 1 WHOLE CHICKEN, FOR EXAMPLE	*TOTAL TIME 5 MINUTES*

Use the lists below and on the right as inspiration, but let the quantities be dictated by what you would like to use up. When I say most things will work well together, I really mean it. My only real advice is to avoid using a whole packet of chilli powder if you don't want your head blown off, but other than that any combination should work.

The lists are all quite long, but you do not need to use such a variety if you only have three or four spices to use up. This is all about experimenting, and you really can't go wrong.

Regarding whole or ground spices, use either. Just watch out for particularly strong spices in ground form (it's probably best to use them sparingly), i.e. cloves, nutmeg, chillies/chiles, peppers, cinnamon, star anise.

Add your chosen spices and herbs to a large mixing bowl, followed by the milk and mix to combine. Add your meat or veg to the marinade and coat (hands are best for this).

SPICED, SMOKEY, EARTHY FLAVOURS

Allspice
Cajun spice
Cayenne pepper
Chilli/hot red pepper flakes
Fennel seeds
Ground coriander
Ground ginger
Mustard powder/seeds
Nigella seeds
Urfa chilli

SOUTH ASIAN FLAVOURS

All curry spice mixes/powders
Caraway seeds
Cardamom pods (bash them to release the seeds)
Chilli/chile
Cinnamon
Cloves
Cumin seeds
Fennel seeds
Garam masala
Garlic
Ground ginger
Ground turmeric
Mustard powder/seeds
Sichuan pepper
Star anise

HERBY, GARLICKY, MEDITERRANEAN FLAVOURS

Aleppo pepper
All green herbs
Bay leaves
Cayenne pepper
Cumin seeds
Dukkah
Fennel seeds
Garlic/garlic granules
Nigella seeds
Paprika
Pink peppercorns
Saffron
Sumac
Za'atar

A REALLY RANDOM, DELICIOUS MARINADE I ONCE MADE, TO SHOW YOU REALLY CAN JUST WING IT!

Black pepper

Cajun spice

Cumin seeds

Garlic granules

Ground ginger

Mustard powder/seeds

Smoked paprika

GOES WELL WITH Very good over chicken, pork, roast vegetables, you name it...

LABNEH

Labneh is a Mediterranean soft cream cheese and it couldn't be simpler to make, the only thing you need is time. It's a great way to use up yogurt that is approaching its use-by date. It takes a day or so to 'make' but the hands-on time is literally about 5 minutes, then it'll last in your fridge for a few weeks. One thing to note: the longer you leave it to 'hang', the thicker it'll become, so play around with that and see what you prefer, which will mirror how you enjoy using it.

500 g/2¼ cups Greek yogurt	Try plain, sheep or goat's yogurt
1 teaspoon sea salt	Sea salt flakes are best, but if using fine, just ½ teaspoon
MAKES 350 G/1¾ CUPS	*TOTAL TIME 5 MINUTES, PLUS HANGING (ABOUT 24–48 HOURS)*

Mix the yogurt and salt together.

Place a sieve/strainer over a large mixing bowl. Lay a clean, tightly woven tea/dish towel (or double layer of muslin/cheesecloth if you have it) on top of the sieve and pour the yogurt into the centre.

Bring the edges of the tea towel together and tie it up securely, with string or an elastic band (I find string is best). Now you need to hang the labneh up somewhere, with the bowl directly below to catch all the drips. I suspend mine from the handle of a kitchen wall cupboard and sit the bowl on the work surface below (see the photo on page 5).

Leave to hang for 24–48 hours, depending on how thick you want it. The looser the yogurt, the longer it will take to strain, so if you've used loose, plain natural yogurt as a substitute, it might be worth waiting closer to 48 hours.

When ready, simply transfer the labneh into a sealable container and store in the fridge. The milky water in the bowl can be discarded.

GOES WELL WITH Labneh is a great savoury addition to lots of dishes – use it as a base for roasted veg on a platter, as a sandwich or wrap spread, as a topping for meatballs, or load it up with some chopped cucumber, herbs, spices, a bit of oil and use it as a dip. Labneh always benefits from a glug of oil and a squeeze of lemon juice, but just see what you like!

LEFTOVERS Just keep using it as above in a variety of dishes – treat it like ricotta or cream cheese and you won't go wrong.

MILK POPS

Mini milks are often my ice lolly/popsicle of choice, as I just love the simplicity of them. They're so delicious! This is my take on them, with a little spicing to tart them up.

2 cardamom pods	Essential
397-g/14-oz can condensed milk	Essential
300 ml/1¼ cups whole milk	Semi-skimmed milk or dairy-free milk
200 ml/1 cup Greek yogurt	Any plain yogurt, but the higher in fat, the better
a good grating of nutmeg	Pinch of ground cinnamon
MAKES 10	*TOTAL TIME 10 MINUTES, PLUS FREEZING*

Ice lolly/popsicle mould and lolly/popsicle sticks

Break the cardamom pods open to reveal the seeds, then grind the seeds using a pestle and mortar.

Add the ground cardamom seeds, condensed milk, milk and yogurt to a high-powered blender (or a standard jug blender). Grate in a generous sprinkling of nutmeg too, then blitz until fully combined.

Taste to check for flavour, and add a little more spice if you wish – remember that the flavours will dull as they freeze, so don't be shy.

Pour the milk pop mix into your ice lolly/popsicle moulds (don't forget to add the sticks), then transfer to the freezer and freeze for 6 hours, or even better, overnight.

GOES WELL WITH A hot day, or a big meal (they're wonderful after a curry).

LEFTOVERS They are very happy in the freezer! Just make sure that once you've removed them from the ice lolly mould, they live in a sealed container. I often place a piece of parchment paper between each milk pop to avoid them sticking together.

BREAD
FROZEN BREADCRUMBS

So many dishes are vastly improved by the addition of a crispy breadcrumb topping or a crunchy coating. Keep a stash of breadcrumbs in the freezer to use when making a gratin, or add them to stuffings, sauces or patties. The possibilities are endless.

bread	Any variety – soft, toasted or defrosted
MAKES ANY QUANTITY YOU WANT	**TOTAL TIME 5 MINUTES**

Place the bread in a food processor and blitz until the bread has broken up into crumbs. I like mine left a little chunky, and you can always re-blitz them later to make them finer if needed. If you don't have a food processor, finely chop with a knife on a cutting board in the old-fashioned way.

Place the breadcrumbs in a sealable freezerproof container and freeze. As more bread becomes stale or unused, blitz it up in the same way and add to the same container.

Use the breadcrumbs straight from frozen to top a gratin or baked dish, within a meat or veggie patty (such as a burger, fish cake, fritter, etc), for stuffing or thickening a sauce, for making a crumble topping, or add them to a frying pan/skillet to crisp up for a garnish. However, it's best to defrost breadcrumbs if you want to make a golden, crispy coating for something like a schnitzel or for the coating of the fishcakes on page 78. Even better, add them to a baking sheet and gently defrost by placing them in an oven preheated to 100°C fan/ 120°C/250°F/Gas ½ for 1 hour. This will remove any excess moisture that's seeped into the crumbs during the freezing process, and you'll have a brilliantly crisp panée crumb.

Don't forget to load up the breadcrumbs with flavour – here are a few ideas, play around with quantities and use what you've got! And see my corn on the cob recipe on page 119 for a side dish or lunch recipe using breadcrumbs for some full recipe inspiration.

Mix frozen breadcrumbs with any of the following, pan fry and sprinkle on top of *PASTA OR ROASTED VEG:*
Fresh thyme leaves
Olives, pitted and chopped
Lemon zest
Anchovies, roughly chopped
Olive oil

Mix frozen breadcrumbs with any of the following and use as a topping for *ANY LASAGNE, AUBERGINE PARMIGIANA OR CAULIFLOWER CHEESE:*
Garlic, peeled and grated
Parmesan, grated
Parsley, roughly chopped
Chives, thinly sliced
Toasted cumin seeds

Mix frozen breadcrumbs with any of the following, fry gently in butter and use as a sweet topping to pile on top of *BAKED OR ROASTED FRUIT,* or fry on their own and *SERVE WITH ICE CREAM:*
Honey
Ground cinnamon
Nutmeg, grated (or ground)
Soft light brown sugar

FRIDGE RAID TOASTIES

You can load most things into a toastie, but I do think it has to have cheese, or some sort of melting/binding ingredient to bring it all together. Here I've shared a couple of my favourite 'fridge raid' toasties – both are staple work-from-home lunches in our house.

RAGÙ TOASTIE	
2 large slices of sturdy bread	Any bread
2 tablespoons mayonnaise	Room-temperature butter
90 g leftover ragù/thick pasta sauce	This can really be anything, just not too loose
½ vine tomato	Any fresh or sun-dried/sun-blush tomato, sliced olives
90 g/3 oz. mozzarella	Any cheese – whatever you have
10 chives	Any fresh herb; parsley or basil work well
SUNDAY ROAST TOASTIE	
2 large slices of sturdy bread	Any bread
2 tablespoons mayonnaise	Room-temperature butter
75 g/2½ oz. Brie	Any cheese – whatever you have
90 g/3 oz. leftover roast meat	Cooked bacon, nut roast or stuffing
90 g/3 oz. roasted carrots	Any roasted veg
1 spring onion/scallion	Just to add freshness; sliced pickles work well
1 tablespoon Dijon mustard	Any mustard or extra condiment of your choice
2 tablespoons cranberry sauce	Any chutney, just something sweet to bring it together
rapeseed/canola oil, for frying	
MAKES 1 LARGE TOASTIE	*TOTAL TIME 10 MINUTES*

Slice and prepare the fillings however you think best, no real precision is needed here, just thinly slice cheese, meat and veg... you can't go wrong! Spread one side of each piece of bread with the mayonnaise, then turn them over (the mayo will be on the outside of the bread for frying, instead of butter). Pile in the fillings, making sure you spread any spreadable items evenly on the inside of each bread slice. Place the second piece of bread on top with the mayo on the outside.

Place a large frying pan/skillet over a medium heat. Add a drizzle of rapeseed/canola oil, and once hot, add the toastie. Place a piece of parchment paper on top of the toastie, then on top of that, place a heavy weight (pestle and mortar, casserole/Dutch oven, griddle pan) to weigh down the toastie and its contents.

Leave to fry on one side for 4 minutes, until golden brown and crisp underneath. Remove the weight and parchment paper, carefully flip the toastie over and return the paper and weight back to their positions. Leave the toastie to fry on the other side for another 3–4 minutes, then remove from the pan, cut in half and eat up.

GOES WELL WITH I like my toasties accompanied by a packet of crisps/ potato chips and a tangerine to finish (yes, just like lunch for a 10-year-old!). But they're also great with a mug of Chipotle Red Pepper Soup (page 107) or Apple and Cumin Slaw (page 162) on the side. For the Sunday roast toastie, if you have any leftover gravy, warm it up and use it as a dipping sauce – it's glorious.

LEFTOVERS There won't be any.

WEEKEND QUESADILLAS

This recipe is basically loaded scrambled eggs sandwiched between two crispy wraps, what's not to like about that? It only uses one pan, and it's a great dish for the whole family, because it's an eat-with-your-hands meal that you can enjoy lounging in the kitchen on Saturday morning, or eating in the car en route to sports matches. It's also good for lunch, and I have definitely made it for supper too... If you are wanting to make more than two quesadillas, simply double the quantities and you're good to go.

40 g/1½ oz. cheese	Any cheese, hard or soft, that you like with eggs
100 g/3½ oz. mushrooms	Any type of mushroom is fine, or try cooked potato
100 g/3½ oz. bacon lardons	Ham or sliced bacon, or omit
50 g/2 oz. spinach	Any quick-wilting greens, or omit
4 eggs	Essential
4 tortilla wraps, 20-cm/8-inch diameter	Essential
olive oil, for frying	
sea salt and freshly ground pepper	
SERVES 2	*TOTAL TIME 25 MINUTES*

Grate the cheese and finely slice the mushrooms. Add a drizzle of oil to a medium or large, non-stick frying pan/skillet and set over a high heat. Once hot, add the mushrooms and fry for 3 minutes, until softening and starting to colour slightly. Add the lardons to the pan and continue to fry for 3–5 minutes until the bacon is golden and the mushrooms are well browned.

Next, add the spinach and stir it through the mushroom mixture until it wilts – this should only take a minute. Scoop all of the cooked items out of the pan and on to a plate, then wipe the pan clean with some paper towel (don't wash it as you're about to use it again).

Next, whisk the eggs in a bowl, season well, then add the mushroom mixture and briefly mix. The residual heat might start to cook the eggs slightly, but that's fine.

The grated cheese is used to create a barrier for the egg mix, so sprinkle the cheese in a 2.5-cm/1-inch thick ring around the edge of two of the tortillas. Place one of these tortillas in the frying pan, spoon half the egg mixture into the centre and spread it up to the ring of cheese. Gently place a second plain tortilla on top and fry for 2–3 minutes, until the egg is starting to set and the base tortilla is crispy. Using a spatula and some confidence, flip the quesadilla over and fry on the other side for 2–3 minutes. Transfer to a board and repeat with the remaining ingredients. To serve, slice up the quesadillas like a pizza and enjoy.

GOES WELL WITH Brown Sauce (page 63).

LEFTOVERS They're really nice reheated – just get the tortilla nice and crisp again in the oven.

WONKY STUFFED FLATBREADS

This recipe has to be one of my favourites in the book, because I just love homemade flatbread. It has the taste of pizza, but is much quicker to make and so satisfying. Here, I've stuffed the dough and turned the flatbreads into a type of calzone, but with a very manageable amount of filling so they're easy to handle and fry. Try my suggested combinations below, or get creative and think of your own fillings. Like lots of recipes in this book, pretty much anything goes, so experiment with whatever is in your fridge!

400 g/3 cups self-raising/rising flour, plus extra for dusting	Wholemeal/whole-wheat self-raising/rising, or plain/all-purpose flour with 2 teaspoons baking powder
400 g/2 scant cups Greek yogurt	Plain yogurt, or watered-down labneh (page 33)
2 teaspoons sea salt	Essential, but can use 1 teaspoon fine salt
2 tablespoons extra virgin olive oil, plus extra to work with	Standard olive oil or rapeseed/canola oil
MAKES 4 LARGE FLATBREADS	*TOTAL TIME 40 MINUTES, PLUS RESTING*

MARGHERITA FILLING (MAKES 1)

80 g/⅔ cup mozzarella, drained and torn

30 g/¼ cup sundried/sun-blush tomatoes, roughly chopped

a couple of stalks of fresh basil, stalks discarded, leaves left whole

CURRY FILLING (MAKES 1)

130 g/4½ oz. leftover curry of any kind (chop any large chunks of meat or veg so the filling heats up evenly)

a handful of coriander/cilantro, roughly chopped

MARMITE FILLING (MAKES 1)

15 g/1 tablespoon butter

15 g/1 tablespoon Marmite/yeast extract

SWEET FILLING (MAKES 1)

30 g/2 tablespoons ricotta

15 g/1 tablespoon jam/preserve (any flavour), or pre-roasted or stewed fruit

a sprinkle of ground cinnamon

Add the flour, yogurt, salt and olive oil to a large mixing bowl and mix the ingredients with a metal spoon – they will start to clump and come together. Oil your hands and bring the dough together fully, and briefly knead in the bowl. You want to collect any flour that's not yet fully incorporated and achieve a smooth dough, but also avoid overworking it. Leave to rest in the bowl for 30 minutes, covered with a tea/dish towel.

Prepare your fillings, by following the preparation instructions given in the ingredients lists. Please note the quantities I've given will each fill one flatbread, so just double/triple/quadruple those quantities, depending on whether you're making a variety of fillings or all four flatbreads with the same filling.

Dust a clean work surface with a little flour and divide the dough equally into 4 pieces. Roll one piece of dough out to roughly a 30–35-cm/12–14-inch diameter circle, 2 mm/⅛ inch thick. Load your chosen filling ingredients onto one half of the flatbread dough (leaving a clear border of 2 cm/¾ inch around the edge), then fold the other half over the filling. Pinch the edges together with your fingers to seal, then gently roll again to bring the flatbread together. If you can, flip it over and gently roll once more, checking the edges are sealed again. This does not need to be neat, just sealed.

Set a large, heavy-based frying pan/skillet over a high heat. Once hot, add the stuffed flatbread and dry-fry until golden brown – this will take 3–4 minutes on each side. While it cooks, you can start rolling and filling the next piece of dough.

Transfer the cooked, stuffed flatbread to a board and cover with a tea/dish towel to keep warm, then repeat with the remaining ingredients. You could also pop them in a low oven (preheated to 80°C fan/100°C/225°F/Gas ¼), whilst you cook the rest, or just slice them up and share as you go.

Please note: If you are using a meat-based sauce (curry, ragù, chilli, for example) as filling, transfer your stuffed flatbreads into a very hot oven (preheated to 220°C fan/240°C/450°F/Gas 8) for 5 minutes after frying but before serving, to make sure that the meat has fully reheated and come up to a safe temperature for consumption.

GOES WELL WITH I love these flatbreads on their own, or they're great treated like a sandwich and served with Apple and Cumin Slaw (page 162), crisps/potato chips or salad. Simple, but delicious.

LEFTOVERS These are great just reheated and cut into wedges. They're really lovely second time around as the flatbread gets much crispier.

PASTRY & POTATOES
GOAT'S CHEESE TART

Savoury tarts are very much like a frittata in my opinion – you can throw almost anything into them. Lovely short pastry and an eggy-milky filling, loaded with whatever herbs, greens, cheeses, meats (and even fish) you might have in the fridge. This recipe is a great opportunity to get inventive. Use a glut of seasonal greens, or clear out the kitchen's limping leftovers. I've chosen some specific ingredients, but by all means use what you have got. I've used pre-made pastry as it's often in my freezer, but feel free to make some from scratch.

320 g/11½ oz. pre-rolled shortcrust pastry	Homemade is great!
1 shallot	Any sort of onion, or omit
3 spring onions/scallions	Any other onion or half a leek, or omit
140 g/5 oz. chard	Any leafy green is great – kale, cavolo nero, spinach…
10 g/⅓ oz. fresh basil	Most leafy herbs work well – parsley, dill, coriander/cilantro
120 g/4½ oz. soft goat's cheese	Any cheese will work, but soft cheese is preferable
2 eggs	Essential, but any size can be used
150 ml/⅔ cup double/heavy cream	Single/light cream, crème fraîche, sour cream, cream cheese, milk
80 ml/⅓ cup whole milk	Any milk you have, doesn't have to be full-fat
olive oil, for frying	
SERVES 4–6	**TOTAL TIME 1¼ HOURS**

23-cm/9-inch tart pan and baking beans

Preheat the oven to 180°C fan/200°C/400°F/Gas 6. Place a large baking sheet in the oven to heat up.

Lay the pre-rolled pastry over the tart pan. Tear off some of the overhanging pastry, roll it into a ball and use it to push the pastry into the inner edges of the tart pan and up the sides. If your pastry sheet doesn't quite cover the entirety of the sides, cut off the section of pastry that overhangs the most and patch it onto the side(s) that need covering. Leave the rest of the overhanging pastry where it is and lightly prick the base of the pastry with a fork.

Scrunch up a large piece of parchment paper, then open it out again (this makes it more pliable). Place the parchment paper over the pastry and gently pour in the baking beans. Place the tart pan on the preheated baking sheet and transfer to the hot oven.

Blind-bake the pastry case for 20 minutes. Remove the pastry case from the oven, lift out the baking beans and parchment paper, then return the now-exposed pastry case to the oven for another 5–10 minutes, until the pastry is baked and has a dry, sandy texture. Remove from the oven and set aside.

If there are visible cracks or thin areas in the pastry case, beat one of the eggs and brush it over any cracks or holes (save the rest of the egg for the filling). Return to the oven for a couple of minutes and this will seal the pastry, ready for the wet filling.

While you're waiting for the pastry to blind bake and/or cool, you can get on with the filling. Quarter lengthways, peel and trim the shallots. Trim and then cut the spring onions/scallions into 6-cm/2½-inch pieces. Pull the stalks off the chard and break into several pieces, so they're not quite so long.

Add a glug of oil to a large frying pan/skillet and once hot, add the prepared onions and chard stalks. Gently fry for 15 minutes, until lightly caramelized and softening. When they've only got a couple of minutes left in the pan, add the chard leaves and let wilt with the onions and chard stalks. Once ready, remove the pan from the heat and let cool. Once cool, tear in the basil (leaves and stalks) and goat's cheese so that all the chunky fillings are in one place, ready to go.

In a jug/pitcher, whisk the eggs, double/heavy cream and milk with some seasoning.

Trim the edges of the cooked and cooled pastry case by running a serrated knife around the edge of the tart pan to release the gnarly extra pastry and create an even edge. Pile in the onion, chard and cheese mixture, then evenly spread it out across the base. Finally pour the egg mixture over the top.

Carefully turn to the oven for a final bake, placing it on the baking sheet on the top shelf for 30 minutes, until just set and lightly golden on top.

Remove from the oven and let sit for 10 minutes before slicing and serving.

GOES WELL WITH It's quite lovely with a spoonful of Date and Nut Chutney (page 62) on the side and some crunchy lettuce.

LEFTOVERS All quiches and savoury tarts are great simply reheated in the oven, in fact I sometimes prefer them second time around as the pastry goes extra crispy.

SOUP PIE

This is a proper 'fridge and cupboard raid' meal created when I had a random selection of things that needed finishing up (double/heavy cream, leftover rice and greens, cherry tomatoes, etc), plus the usual staples of red lentils, garlic, rosemary from the garden and some bits in the freezer, including filo/phyllo pastry. I'd never made a really soupy pie before – usually you'd have a creamier or thicker consistency for a pie filling, but I just loved how this came out and a crispy filo topping in any situation is always welcome in my house!

80 g/3 oz. carrots	Onion, fennel, more celery, celeriac/celery root, potato, leeks
1 celery stick/stalk	Onion, fennel, more carrot, celeriac/celery root, potato, leeks
a drizzle of olive oil	A flavourless oil
200 g/7 oz. smoked bacon lardons	Unsmoked, pancetta, back bacon, leftover chicken, beef, pork, prawns/shrimp, or omit
2 garlic cloves	Chopped, lazy, purée. If using garlic granules or powder, ½ teaspoon is plenty
3 sprigs of fresh rosemary	Thyme, oregano, sage – a couple pinches of any dried herb (but fresh is best)
250 g/9 oz. fresh mixed cherry tomatoes	Any fresh tomatoes. Canned cherry tomatoes work, or try mushrooms
40 ml/2½ tablespoons red wine vinegar	White wine, cider, sherry vinegar or a splash of white wine or cider
700 ml/3 cups chicken stock	Any stock you have, apart from fish stock
3 balls of frozen spinach	Fresh spinach is great, or green beans, chard, cavolo nero, kale...
80 g/3 oz. frozen greens: peas and edamame	I always have these in the freezer. Or if the season permits, fresh peas
80 g/½ cup red lentils	Cooked lentils or any grain, dried or cooked (if using cooked, add with leftover rice)
50 g/½ cup leftover rice (optional)	Optional (I had some so added it in, but same rules as above: no rule!)
100 g/3½ oz. leftover chopped veg	Optional, but a great way of using up any cooked veg
100 ml/½ cup double/heavy cream	Single/light cream, crème fraîche, sour cream, mascarpone, cream cheese, milk
12–16 sheets filo/phyllo pastry	Essential, but puff (or rough puff) pastry would work
100 g/7 tablespoons butter	Any flavourless oil
sea salt and freshly ground pepper	
SERVES 4	*TOTAL TIME 1 HOUR*

4 x 20-cm/8-inch pie dishes (or two larger ones)

Preheat the oven to 180°C fan/200°C/400°F/Gas 6.

Thinly slice the carrots and celery. Add a small drizzle of olive oil to a large saucepan set over a medium heat and once hot, add the smoked bacon lardons. Fry for 5–7 minutes, until they start to caramelize and turn golden, then add the carrots and celery and fry for another 5 minutes, stirring frequently.

Thinly slice the garlic and strip the rosemary leaves from their stalks, roughly chopping the leaves. Add them both to the pan for 2 minutes (or until fragrant), then add the fresh tomatoes and red wine vinegar and let bubble for a couple of minutes. Add the chicken stock, along with the frozen spinach, frozen greens, lentils and any leftover grains or veg you're throwing in too.

Stir the concoction to combine and bring to the boil. Once bubbling, remove from the heat and pour in the cream and a good pinch of seasoning. Taste to check if you need to season more, then transfer into your pie dishes. I like making this in individual dishes because of the soupiness, but one or two sharing dishes works too.

On a clean work surface, lay out your first filo/phyllo pastry sheet. Melt the butter in the microwave (or in a small saucepan on the hob/stovetop) and liberally brush the entire pastry sheet with the melted butter. Lift it up, scrunch it together and pop it on top of the soup pie mix in one corner. Take another sheet, repeat the butter-brushing process and place it next to the first scrunched up sheet. With the pie dish sizes, I've suggested 3 scrunched-up sheets should be enough to cover one pie, but use as many as you need. Cover the other pies with the remaining sheets, having buttered those too.

Place the filled pie dishes on a baking sheet and bake on the top shelf of the preheated oven for 30 minutes, until crisp, golden brown and smelling amazing. You can also put them in the fridge, pre-oven cooking, and bake later (or the next day).

GOES WELL WITH Seasonal greens, skin-on mashed potato or just on their own.

LEFTOVERS Whilst it's not inventive, this is best just re-heated. Make sure you bring everything right up to temperature, particularly if you have any rice in the pie, so I'd suggest covering the tops of the pies with foil to avoid burnt pastry.

LOADED POTATO SKINS

Who doesn't like baked potatoes? This is a pimped up, twice-baked, but very simple baked potato. I tend to use it as an opportunity to sort out the dairy items in my fridge, so you should too. I have kept this recipe vegetarian, but you could add some crispy bacon to the mix if you wish, for a bit of a salty crunch. However, do as you please and enjoy!

2 large baking potatoes	Smaller or sweet potatoes, squash or celeriac/celery root
6 spring onions/scallions	Chives, finely chopped shallot or red onion (use half if raw)
150 g/scant ¾ cup cream cheese	Crème fraîche, sour cream, buttermilk, double/heavy cream
a good splash of whole milk – about 80 ml/⅓ cup	Any milk that you have is fine
100 g/½ cup pesto	Chimichurri, salsa verde, any herby sauce, lots of fresh herbs
100 g/3½ oz. cheese (Parmesan, Cheddar, Gouda, mozzarella)	A mixture is good, just use what you've got
sea salt	
rapeseed/canola oil, for baking	
SERVES 2 (OR 4 AS A SIDE)	*TOTAL TIME 2 HOURS*

Preheat the oven to 220°C fan/240°C/450°F/Gas 8. Carefully stab the potatoes with a sharp knife, then rub in a little oil and salt. Place on a baking sheet and pop on the top shelf of the preheated oven. Bake for 1½ hours.

About 10 minutes before the potatoes have had their time, trim and slice the spring onions/scallions and add to a large mixing bowl with the cream cheese, milk and pesto. Grate in all of the cheese. Feel free to add any herbs, chopped olives or extra bits and bobs (such as cooked ham, bacon, tuna, other veg, etc) to the bowl if you wish. Season very well and set aside.

Remove the potatoes from the oven. Holding them with a tea/dish towel, cut in half and scoop the flesh straight into the mixing bowl. Roughly mash the ingredients together, then pile back into the skins and place back on the baking sheet. Return to the oven for 20 minutes, until golden, bubbling and ready to devour. Serve immediately.

GOES WELL WITH Brown Sauce (page 63) and for a big meal, the Bavette Steak with Romesco (page 145).

LEFTOVERS Sliced up and fried for a cheesy bubble and squeak is great, or chop it up and make cheesy potato cakes in a frying pan/skillet, topped with an egg and some bacon for a brilliant weekend brunch.

KITCHEN
CONDIMENTS

CANNED OLIVE TAPENADE

Tapenade is a brilliant spread to whip up in minutes, ideal when you have people coming over and no nibbles at home. I used to make it on catering jobs and serve it on grilled sourdough crostinis with evening drinks before dinner, but it's also really nice served simply toast or crackers. Make a batch and keep it in the fridge ready to use for snacks, as a dollop on your fried egg, to add to a sandwich with tomatoes and mozzarella, to fold a spoonful into a ragù for a savoury tang, or simply to enjoy alongside crusty bread and a good, strong cheese. This recipe doesn't have a huge amount of alternative options as it is fairly specific, but hopefully you'll have them in stock as they are pretty much all store-cupboard items.

2 anchovies, drained	Fairly essential, but can be omitted
1 tablespoon capers, drained	Caperberries or drained cornichons
1 garlic clove, peeled	Essential
5 g/¼ oz. parsley	Can be omitted
½ lemon	Fairly essential
3 tablespoons extra virgin olive oil	Normal olive oil is fine
170 g/6 oz. canned or jarred olives (drained weight)	I use black canned or jarred pitted olives. Also try it with green olives
a good pinch of ground black pepper	Essential
SERVES 6–8	**TOTAL TIME 5 MINUTES**

Add the anchovies, capers, garlic, parsley and lemon (zest and juice) and 1 tablespoon of the oil to a food processor and blitz to combine. Next, add the olives, give them a blitz, then gradually pour in the rest of the oil along with a good pinch of black pepper. I prefer not to be too generous with the blitzing time as I like the tapenade to be a bit chunky – like most things it benefits from retaining some texture, but you can have it smooth if you wish.

Taste to check for seasoning, then serve.

GOES WELL WITH See suggestions above, but spread onto crackers or crostini, it's also really great as a garnish for eggs, soup, whatever you like.

LEFTOVERS As this is a kind of dip, it can be used in plenty of ways to mix things up (see recipe introduction). Or try adding small spoons of it to a frittata or quiche so you get small umami nuggets through each slice. Store in the fridge for about 5 days.

HERB & ROMAINE SAUCE

This is a very useful and flavoursome sauce, which uses up limp lettuce and wilting herbs, all brought together into a creamy, lemon sauce. It goes wonderfully with fish or chicken, but my favourite way to enjoy it is to douse pasta in a plentiful amount of the smooth sauce. It freezes well, so if some lettuce needs using, make the sauce, then freeze for a no-fuss dinner in a few weeks' time.

1 onion	A leek or ½ a celery stick/stalk
2 garlic cloves	Garlic purée or ¼ teaspoon garlic powder
150 g/5½ oz. cos/romaine or Little Gem/Boston lettuce	Any lettuce or spinach
5 g/¼ oz. parsley	Tarragon, coriander/cilantro, a little dill or basil
50 ml/3½ tablespoons white wine	White wine vinegar or 25 ml/5 teaspoons cider vinegar
80 ml/⅓ cup double/heavy cream	Single/light cream, crème fraîche or whole milk
50 ml/3½ tablespoons water	
freshly squeezed juice of ½ a lemon	Lime
butter, for frying	
sea salt and freshly ground pepper	
SERVES 4	**TOTAL TIME 25 MINUTES**

Halve, peel and thinly slice the onion. Peel and grate the garlic.

Add a generous knob/pat of butter to a medium saucepan set over a medium heat, and once the butter is melted and gently sizzling, add the onion. Gently fry for 10 minutes, stirring often, until softening and starting to caramelize a little.

Meanwhile, thinly slice the lettuce and herbs. Next, add the garlic and lettuce to the pan and briefly fry for 4 minutes. Add the wine and let it bubble until it has almost all been absorbed, then pour in the cream and water. Squeeze in the lemon juice and bring to the boil. Reduce the heat, season and let the chunky sauce simmer gently for 5 minutes.

Add the herbs, then whizz the sauce with a stick/immersion blender. You can also add it to a high-powered blender if you prefer a really smooth sauce, which I do for this recipe. If so, let it cool down for a couple of minute before you seal the blender. Taste to check for seasoning once more and serve.

GOES WELL WITH Plain rice and roast or poached chicken. Or my favourite, with pasta and some Parmesan.

LEFTOVERS Blitzed into a soup! It's really lovely, especially with good chicken stock and even some shredded chicken. If you only have a small amount of leftover sauce, use it as a dip with some crudités, but it might benefit from some seasoned yogurt to bulk it up.

HAL'S YOGURT & TAHINI DRESSING

Hal, my husband, doesn't get a lot of air time in the 'creation wing' of the kitchen, as I'm afraid that is fairly dominated by me, but this is a lovely dressing that he whipped up. This is one of my favourites during the warmer months, because it is not only very moreish, but it's really very versatile. It's punchy though, so be ready for a hit of flavour. See below for some ideas on how and what you might serve it with.

1 small garlic clove	Flavoursome, but can be omitted
50 g/¼ cup Greek yogurt	Natural, plain yogurt
40 g/scant ¼ cup tahini	Essential
10 g/2 teaspoons Dijon mustard	Any type of mustard
5 g/1 teaspoon honey	Agave, date syrup, golden caster/granulated or any brown sugar
freshly squeezed juice of 2 lemons	2–3 limes
1 tablespoon water	
sea salt and freshly ground pepper	
MAKES 150 ML/⅔ CUP	*TOTAL TIME 5 MINUTES*

Peel and grate the garlic clove.

Whisk all the ingredients together in a bowl. Alternatively, blitz in a high-powered blender. Taste and season, then generously pour over whatever you're serving.

GOES WELL WITH It is so delicious as a thick dressing for a crunchy salad (you might want to thin it out a bit with some water), over roasted or barbecued veg, with cooked grains, you name it. If you double up the yogurt and make it thicker, it's great as a dip for pizzas or flatbreads, too.

LEFTOVERS Just store it in the fridge and slather it over your next meal.

CONFIT GARLIC

If you make no other condiment, make this one. Confit garlic also makes a great homemade gift. I've jotted down lots of ideas for its use at the bottom of the page, but I tend to add mine to 90% of the food I make at home, so you can't go too wrong. Enjoy!

3 garlic bulbs	Essential
200 ml/¾ cup olive oil	Rapeseed/canola oil
1 rosemary stalk	Any hardy herb is lovely here, dried chilli/chile too
1 bay leaf	Any hardy herb is lovely here, whole spices too
FILLS 1 X 370-ML/12½-OZ. JAM JAR	*TOTAL TIME 50 MINUTES*

Sterilized jam jar (see page 10 for how to sterilize) or sealable container

Peel all of the garlic cloves... a daunting task, but it's well worth the 10 minutes of effort and it is also much better to do it now, rather than having skins floating around in the garlic jar later. If you're struggling, add a small handful of cloves (skin-on) into a jar, shake it around vigorously and once opened, the skins will be looser, and much easier to tear off.

Add all the peeled garlic cloves to a small saucepan, along with the olive oil, rosemary and bay. Place over the lowest heat possible and let very, very gently confit for 40 minutes. You don't want even as much as a simmer and certainly not a boil. A good way to keep the pan temperature very low is to have the pan half off the heat source so it has even less direct heat. You can also remove the pan from the heat completely, to let it cool down a bit, then return to the hob/stovetop. The aim is to see occasional, tiny little bubbles, but nothing more.

The confit garlic is ready when the cloves are tender, but remain uncoloured. Remove the pan from the heat and transfer the garlic and herbs in their oil to a sterilized jar. Once cool, seal and store in the fridge. As long as the garlic cloves are submerged in oil they will last for ages (but you'll soon use them up because they're so delicious).

The oil will firm up while stored in the fridge, so just leave the jar out at room temperature for an hour before lunch, supper... and even breakfast.

GOES WELL WITH Add them to sauces, sandwiches, dressings, serve them on top of eggs, in stir fries, on toast with butter (seriously), fold into pasta sauces or ragùs or risottos, the options are endless. Make sure you save the garlic oil too – use it for gentle frying, but it's best for dressings or drizzlings. It's so good!

LEFTOVERS As shown above, you can add confit garlic (and its oil) to a multitude of things.

DATE & NUT CHUTNEY

I swear I always have a punnet of dates in my fridge... They're not even meant to live in there, but I have always done so and they seem to last forever. So, when the time comes for that spot in the fridge to be cleared, I make this chutney and the dates live on. It's a great store-cupboard recipe, needing nothing fresh apart from the ginger.

300 g/2¼ cups pitted dates	Any dates! Dried apricots are nice, or a mix of dried and fresh
1 red onion	Any onion or shallot
60-g/2¼-oz. piece of fresh ginger	30 g/2 tablespoons ginger purée
100 g/3½ oz. nuts	Any nuts – I use half pecans, half walnuts
150 ml/⅔ cup red wine vinegar	Any vinegar – cider or white wine are the best alternatives
50 g/¼ cup demerara/turbinado sugar	Ideally any brown sugar, but white can be used
1 teaspoon caraway seeds	Fennel seeds or ½ teaspoon cumin seeds
1 teaspoon mustard seeds	Any colour is fine, or crushed coriander seeds
400 ml/1¾ cups water	Essential
SERVES 8–10	*TOTAL TIME 45 MINUTES*

2–3 clean, sterilized jam jars (see page 10 for how to sterilize)

Halve the dates. Halve, peel and chop the onion into 1–2-cm/½–¾-inch pieces. Chop the ginger into matchsticks (no need to peel).

Add all the ingredients to a medium saucepan and bring to the boil. Once boiling, cover with a lid, reduce the heat to a gentle simmer and leave to cook slowly for 40 minutes, until thick, sticky and glossy. Make sure you stir the pan occasionally. If at any point it looks as though it's drying out, add a splash of water to the pan.

Remove the pan from the heat, let it cool for 10 minutes, then spoon the chutney into sterilized jars and store for months! Once opened, store in the fridge and use within a month.

GOES WELL WITH Some cheese and crackers or my Hunk of Cheese Scones (page 26).

LEFTOVERS This is a simple preserve-style recipe, so you don't need to eat it all up at once. It makes a lovely gift too.

BROWN SAUCE

This sauce is my favourite condiment. I think it's a nostalgia thing – it's my parents' favourite and takes me back to eating bacon sandwiches at the weekend when growing up. The sauce will happily live in the fridge for up to 6 months, so just make sure you sterilize the jars properly – the best and easiest way is just to run them through the dishwasher.

1 onion	A large shallot or some celery
200 g/7 oz. apples	Pear, or more tomatoes
30 g/1 oz. piece of fresh ginger	2 teaspoons ground ginger
300 g/10½ oz. fresh tomatoes	Good-quality canned tomatoes
100 g/¾ cup pitted dates	Prunes
60 ml/4 tablespoons apple juice	Pear juice, or water plus 1 tablespoon sugar
1 chilli/chile	¼ teaspoon dried chilli/hot red pepper flakes
½ teaspoon fennel seeds	Cumin seeds, or omit
1 teaspoon ground allspice	Mixed spice
500 ml/2 cups water	
150 ml/⅔ cup red wine vinegar	Any vinegar, eg white, cider, sherry
2 tablespoons Worcestershire sauce	No real substitute; omit if necessary
100 g/½ cup demerara/turbinado sugar	Any brown sugar
3 tablespoons tamarind paste	Juice of 1 lime plus 1 tablespoon sugar
olive oil, for frying	
sea salt and freshly ground pepper	
MAKES ABOUT 900 ML/4 CUPS	*TOTAL TIME 1½ HOURS*

clean, sterilized jam jars (see page 10 for how to sterilize)

Add a drizzle of oil to a medium saucepan set over a medium heat and while it heats up, halve, peel and thinly slice the onion. Once the pan is hot, add the onion and let it gently fry for 10 minutes, stirring often, until softening and slightly caramelized.

Core the apple, then finely chop along with the ginger (no need to peel either of them). Roughly chop the tomatoes and dates. Trim and de-seed the chillies/chiles. Add all the remaining ingredients to the pan with a generous pinch of seasoning and bring the mixture to the boil. Once bubbling, reduce the heat to a gentle simmer, and let gently bubble for 1 hour.

Let the mix cool slightly, then transfer to a high-powered blender or food processor and blitz until smooth. Season again, very well. Don't be shy, the flavours can take (and need) salt to even everything out. Pour into sterilized bottles and store in the fridge.

GOES WELL WITH Obviously the best pairing is with a bacon sandwich, but also so many other things. Try it with the Weekend Quesadillas (page 41).

LEFTOVERS It can live in the fridge for up to 6 months, so just use it as and when you like.

TARTARE SAUCE

Traditionally tartare is served with fish, and rightly so, but I also love it with roasted veg, with chicken or as a side at barbecue feasts. Make it as I have done using the ingredients below, or pile in any fresh herbs you've got. I really like cooked onion in a tartare too, which I guess makes it 'not' a tartare, but it's lovely all the same.

10 g/1 tablespoon shallot	Such a tiny amount, so you can omit
10 g/1 tablespoon capers	Double up the cornichons if you don't have capers
20 g/2 tablespoons cornichons	Double up the capers if you don't have cornichons
5 g/3 tablespoons fresh dill (hardy stalks discarded)	Use parsley or coriander/cilantro
zest and freshly squeezed juice of 1 lemon	Ideally use lemon, but use lime if you wish
200 g/1 scant cup Greek yogurt	Plain, natural yogurt (dairy-free if needed too)
sea salt and freshly ground pepper	
SERVES 4–6	*TOTAL TIME 5 MINUTES*

Halve, peel and very finely chop the shallot, roughly chop the capers and cornichons and roughly chop the dill. Add all of the prepared ingredients to a cereal bowl, along with the lemon zest and the yogurt.

Also add a generous pinch of pepper, a good squeeze of lemon juice, then taste again and season more, if you wish, with sea salt and more lemon juice.

GOES WELL WITH Loads of dishes, not just fish! I love it with the Hunk of Cheese Scones (page 26) and the Loaded Potato Skins (page 53). It's also lovely with roast chicken, roasted veg and barbecue spreads.

LEFTOVERS Goes really well with the Spring Onion and Sweetcorn Fritters (page 73) as a dip.

CORIANDER & CHILLI SAUCE

This is such a winning condiment, it goes with so many dishes and it is my favourite way to use up a bunch of coriander/cilantro that's past its best. Chillies/chiles, by the way, live very happily in the freezer, so next time you buy a few but don't use them straight away, pop them in a freezer bag and you'll always have one ready to make this lovely sauce. I've listed some ideas below for what you might enjoy it with, too. Beware that this sauce is quite hot, so if you don't love really spicy/hot sauces, de-seed the chilli before using.

1 garlic clove	½ teaspoon garlic purée
1 jalapeño chilli/chile	Any type of chilli/chile, but preferably green
45 g/1½ oz. fresh coriander/cilantro	Parsley, or a combination of soft herbs
1 vine tomato	A squeeze of lime juice
1 teaspoon red wine vinegar	Any vinegar
5 tablespoons water	
¼ teaspoon sea salt	A pinch of table salt is fine
MAKES 150 ML/5 OZ.	**TOTAL TIME 5 MINUTES**

Peel the garlic and trim the stalk off the chilli/chile.

Add all the ingredients to a food processor and pulse until very finely chopped. If you prefer a smooth sauce, blend further. You can also make it in a high-powered blender and create a fully smooth sauce – it's really up to you!

Store in the fridge for up to 4 days.

GOES WELL WITH So many things! I love it with tacos as a spicy garnish, and it's also great with the Chorizo and Butter Bean Chilli (page 71) or with steak as a kind of chimichurri.

LEFTOVERS Store in the fridge and use it as a warming but fresh addition to lots of meals. Great with eggs.

SPRING

CHICKENY-GREENY-SAUCY ONE-PAN PASTA

Who doesn't love a creamy pasta partnered with torn chicken and fresh greens?
The ingredients below are simply what I had to hand at the time, but there are so
many alternatives.

200 g/7 oz. Tenderstem broccoli/ broccolini	Standard broccoli, green beans, Brussels sprouts or any leafy greens
2 garlic cloves	Garlic purée or chopped garlic
200 g/7 oz. cooked chicken	Bacon, Parma ham or any cured pork (but ½ quantity), pork or prawns/shrimp
900 ml/4 scant cups boiling water	
1 chicken stock jelly	Vegetable stock jelly or cube
160 g/5½ oz. dried pasta	Any sort of pasta you have
100 g/¾ cup frozen peas	Fresh peas, edamame, sweetcorn, kale, asparagus
150 g/¾ cup crème fraîche	Single/light cream, double/heavy cream, sour cream, mascarpone, milk
freshly squeezed juice of 1 lemon	A dash of white wine vinegar
30 g/⅓ cup Parmesan	Any hard cheese will do
10 g/⅓ oz. fresh mint, stalks discarded	Basil, parsley, coriander/cilantro or thyme (if thyme, add with garlic)
olive oil, for cooking	
sea salt and freshly ground pepper	
SERVES 2	*TOTAL TIME 25 MINUTES*

Slice the broccoli stems into 3 or 4 pieces, then peel and thinly slice the garlic.

Add a drizzle of oil to a large, high-sided frying pan/skillet set over a medium heat. When hot, add the chicken and garlic and fry for 5 minutes, stirring very often to avoid the garlic burning. Next, add the water, stock jelly and pasta to the pan with a generous pinch of seasoning. Bring to the boil, cover with a lid and let bubble away for 8 minutes.

When there are only 4 minutes of cooking time left, add the greens (peas and broccoli), stir in and replace the lid. You might need to increase the heat slightly to get the temperature back up to a good bubble. Add a splash more water if the pasta is looking in need. After 4 minutes, remove the lid and reduce the heat to low, then add the crème fraîche and stir in. Taste to check for seasoning. Remove the pan from the heat and add the lemon juice, Parmesan and mint leaves. Stir well, then pile into bowls, making sure you pour all the soupy sauce in too. Finish with extra Parmesan if you like.

GOES WELL WITH You don't need anything – it's full of sauciness, greens, chicken and pasta.

LEFTOVERS Great reheated with a handful of fresh spinach, or turn it into a pasta bake with some more pasta to bulk it out, and a cheesy breadcrumb topping.

CHORIZO & BUTTER BEAN CHILLI WITH LEAFY GREENS, YOGURT & HERBS

This is my go-to recipe when there's not a huge amount of fresh produce in the house, but we want something saucy, full of flavour and comforting, yet 'bright'. The only fresh items are in the serving ingredients, but these can be chopped and changed – as I hope you're learning, I'm not precious about these things. The chilli can be made with any canned (or soaked and simmered) beans, any sort of cured pork product, but my favourite combination is butter/lima beans and chorizo. This is a real winner and the leftovers are almost better than the first sitting. If you're cooking for children, omit the cayenne pepper and have it to hand to sprinkle over the grown-ups' bowls when you serve.

225 g/9 oz. chorizo	Bacon, salami, any cured meat, also great with chicken
2 red onions	Any type of onion, leek or fennel
5 garlic cloves	You need these, but purée can be substituted
1 teaspoon smoked paprika	Sweet paprika is fine, or maybe try some dried herbs
½ teaspoon cayenne pepper	Dried chilli powder, chilli/hot red pepper flakes or more paprika is fine
100 ml/⅓ cup plus 1 tablespoon whIte wIne	Red wine is fine, or use white or red wine vinegar
60 g/⅓ cup red split lentils	Any lentils will work, or more beans
400-g/14-oz. can of cooked butter/ lima beans, drained and rinsed	Any cooked, drained beans work
2 x 400-g/14-oz. cans of tomatoes	You need these, or use passata/strained tomatoes or fresh tomatoes
30 g/1 oz. fresh soft mixed herbs	Parsley, coriander/cilantro, basil, chives, dill or mint
1 lime	Lemon can be used
500 g/1 lb. 2 oz. spring greens	Any cabbage-style greens work well, or just salad!
150 g/¾ cup plain yogurt	Any type of unflavoured/plain yogurt or sour cream
olive oil, for cooking	
butter, for frying	
salt and freshly ground black pepper	
SERVES 4	*TOTAL TIME 1 HOUR 10 MINUTES*

Thinly slice the chorizo into 5-mm/¼-inch pieces. Add a glug of oil to a casserole dish/ Dutch oven set over a medium heat. Once hot, add the chorizo and fry for 5 minutes, stirring regularly.

GOES WELL WITH Either of the sides I have suggested or, of course, with steamed rice. It's lovely with the Coriander and Chilli Sauce (page 65) as an extra garnish too.

LEFTOVERS Great piled into wraps or tacos with some fried halloumi, on toast with eggs, turned into a shakshuka base or even in a cheese toastie.

Halve, peel and slice the onions. Peel and thinly slice the garlic. Once the chorizo is crisping up and glistening after 5 minutes, add the onions to the dish and fry for a further 15 minutes, until softening and laced with orange oil. Stir often to avoid burning.

After 15 minutes, add the garlic, paprika and cayenne pepper and stir them into the mix, then cook them for 2 minutes, until fragrant. Next, add the wine and let it bubble away, until the liquid has almost completely reduced. Add the lentils, drained butter/lima beans and tomatoes to the dish, then refill one empty tomato can with water and pour that in too. Bring up to the boil, season well, then reduce the heat to a gentle simmer and leave to bubble gently on the hob/stovetop for 40 minutes.

Tear or roughly chop the herbs and mix in a bowl, then lightly season and squeeze over the juice of half the lime, set aside. Cut the remaining lime half into wedges.

When the chilli has only 5 minutes left to cook, thickly slice the spring greens, thinly slice the base (don't discard it!) and heat a knob/pat of butter in a large frying pan/skillet. Once it's sizzling, add the greens, along with a good splash of water and a pinch of seasoning. Let them steam/fry for 5 minutes, until softening and tender but still with a bite.

Taste the chilli one final time and season again (it'll probably need it). Pile the chilli into bowls alongside the wilted greens and top with a dollop of yogurt, followed by a handful of herb salad and a wedge of lime on the side for squeezing over.

SPRING ONION & SWEETCORN FRITTERS

Sweetcorn fritters are good at any time of the day in my opinion. I love this combination, too – oniony, sweet with a little heat, and they go perfectly with my Tartare Sauce or a good garlicky yogurt dip. They're very moreish, so you might actually want to double the quantities and make more. We never have any leftovers and I'm often eating them before they even get to the table! Use the swap-in options and play around, like usual.

6 spring onions/scallions	Thinly sliced shallot, or any raw leafy green, thinly sliced
1 green chilli/chile	Any fresh chilli/chile, or use ½–1 teaspoon dried chilli/hot red pepper flakes
20 g/¾ oz. coriander/cilantro	Any fresh soft herb, or a mixture
190-g/7-oz. can of sweetcorn/corn kernels (160 g/5½ oz. drained weight)	Try halved cherry tomatoes, chickpeas, or more spring onions/scallions
2 eggs	Essential
50 ml/3½ tablespoons milk	Any kind of milk, or a dollop of yogurt
2 garlic cloves	Great for flavour but not essential; purée is fine
1 teaspoon dried dill	Great for flavour but not essential; try fresh dill or basil
60 g/scant ½ cup plain/all-purpose flour	Any flour will do; if using self-raising/rising omit the baking powder
1 teaspoon baking powder	Not essential, can omit
350 ml/1½ cups rapeseed/canola oil	You need an oil with a high burning-point, such as vegetable or sunflower oil
sea salt and freshly ground pepper	
SERVES 3–4	*TOTAL TIME 50 MINUTES*

Trim, then thinly slice the spring onions/scallions. Trim, halve, de-seed (if you wish) and thinly slice the chilli/chile. Roughly chop the coriander/cilantro (along with its stalks). Drain the canned sweetcorn/corn kernels.

Break the eggs into a large mixing bowl and add the milk. Scatter in a generous pinch of seasoning. Peel the garlic, then grate this in too, and briefly whisk with a fork to combine. Next, add all the prepared veg and herbs (including the dried dill) to the egg mixture and season very well. Add in the flour and baking powder, and using a metal spoon, fold together to coat and combine. You don't want to overwork the mixture, but the flour does need to be fully incorporated – the mixture should be thick, but sloppy.

Pour the oil into a large frying pan/skillet to the depth of about 3 mm/⅛ inch (so you may need less than the amount I've specified above if you're using a smaller pan).

Place the pan over a medium heat – you'll know the oil is hot enough when you drop a small amount of fritter mixture into the pan and it sizzles immediately. Bear in mind, though, that you don't want the oil to overheat, so if you notice the fritters are colouring very quickly, turn it down slightly. Also remember that when you start adding the fritters to the pan, the temperature of the oil will drop, so just go gently and keep an eye on it.

Once the oil is ready, add a few heaped tablespoons of fritter mixture to the pan. Cook the fritters in batches to avoid overcrowding the pan and make sure there's 2.5 cm/1 inch or so of space between each fritter pile.

Fry for about 3–5 minutes on each side, just until they are golden brown and crispy. Once done, transfer them to a plate lined with paper towels or to a cooling rack (placed above a tray). Repeat with the remaining fritter mixture until it has all been used.

GOES WELL WITH Try these with my Tartare Sauce (page 64) or just some well-seasoned yogurt.

LEFTOVERS These store well in the fridge for a couple days, then re-heat them in the oven. They can also be frozen (to reheat the fritters, defrost, then place on a baking sheet, cover with foil and cook in an oven preheated to 180°C fan/200°C/400°F/Gas 6 for 15 minutes or until piping hot).

GOES WELL WITH You don't need anything with these noodles, they're full of umami and really flavoursome; however a cold beer wouldn't go amiss!

LEFTOVERS Reheat in a large hot frying pan/skillet with a good drizzle of sesame oil and some extra greens to bulk it out. Some crispy bacon, leftover chicken or more tofu is great, too.

TOFU NOODLES WITH MUSHROOMS & MARMITE

It may sound weird to add Marmite/yeast extract to noodles and tofu, but honestly, it's really delicious and not overpowering. Marmite (which I love) adds some umami or savoury depth without any effort at all. Even if you don't like Marmite, you will still enjoy this recipe.

3 garlic cloves	Purée, lazy garlic or ½ teaspoon garlic powder
30-g/1-oz. piece of fresh ginger	Purée, or omit
1 red chilli/chile	Any chilli/chile is fine here, chilli/hot red pepper flakes or powder too, but use less
200 g/7 oz. mushrooms	Any type of mushrooms, chicken or bacon
225 g/8 oz. smoked tofu (I use Tofoo)	Plain tofu is fine, but smoked is more flavoursome
100 g/3½ oz. greens	Pak choi/bok choi, purple sprouting broccoli, kale, spinach, anything!
2 tablespoons sesame oil	Sesame oil is great, but any oil to loosen up is ok
1 tablespoon Marmite/yeast extract	Bovril or Vegemite
1 tablespoon rice vinegar	Any vinegar, such as white wine, cider or red wine (but nothing too strong)
300 g/10½ oz. udon noodles	Any pre-made noodles that only need a flash in a pan to heat
1 lime, cut into wedges	Lemon would be ok, but lime is best, or omit
rapeseed/canola oil, for frying	
sea salt and freshly ground pepper	

SERVES 2　　　　**TOTAL TIME 30 MINUTES**

Peel and thinly slice the garlic. Trim, then cut the ginger into matchsticks. Trim, then thinly slice the chilli/chile. Thickly slice the mushrooms. Cut the tofu into 2-cm/¾-inch cubes. Slice the greens into long, slim pieces; halve any purple sprouting broccoli (lengthways too if they're quite thick), thickly slice any leafy greens, leave spinach or kale whole, cut pak choi into thirds.

Add a glug of oil to large frying pan/skillet set over a medium-high heat and once hot, add the tofu cubes and fry them for about 10 minutes until golden on all sides, turning often. Transfer the golden tofu to a plate.

Pile the garlic, ginger, chilli and mushrooms into the pan. Fry for 5 minutes until softening and slightly browned. Add the greens and toss to combine, letting them wilt and briefly cook for 2 minutes. Return the tofu to the pan and add the sesame oil, Marmite/yeast extract and vinegar. Stir to mix all the ingredients together, then push them to the sides of the pan to create a gap in the centre. Tip the noodles into the gap so they have direct contact with the base of the pan. Leave for 30 seconds, then start to jiggle them a bit to help them loosen up. Toss all the ingredients together for a couple of minutes until piping hot and fully combined. Finish with a good squeeze of lime juice, season and remove from the heat. Serve immediately.

SALMON & SUMAC FISHCAKES

This is a great recipe to whip up when you know you've got salmon, potatoes and breadcrumbs, as you can then figure out the rest according to what you can find in the kitchen. The fishcakes have some lovely pops of flavour due to the herbs, spring onions/ scallions and cornichons they contain, but those can be swapped out for other things – have a look below and get gathering your ingredients...

250 g/9 oz. potatoes	Any good all-rounder variety
1 tablespoon whole milk	Any milk, even dairy-free
250 g/9 oz. sustainable salmon, skinless and boneless	Any sustainable fish that you might add to a fish pie is fine
1 lemon	Not essential, but it's a great addition
20 g/¾ oz. each parsley and dill	Any soft herb – coriander/cilantro, basil, more dill...
20 g/¾ oz. cornichons	Capers, olives, larger pickles chopped up
2 spring onions/scallions	Raw shallot or red onion, finely chopped
2½ teaspoons sumac	More lemon zest if you have some, or omit
3 tablespoons plain/all-purpose flour	Any flour
1 egg, whisked	The egg is ideal but use milk if you don't have one
60 g/¾ cup plain breadcrumbs	Essential, can use panko or dried
200 ml/¾ cup oil, for frying	Any flavourless oil with a high burning point
sea salt and freshly ground pepper	
MAKES 4 FISHCAKES	*TOTAL TIME 45 MINUTES*

Chop the potatoes (skin on) into 3-cm/1¼-inch pieces. Bring a medium pan of salted water to the boil, then add the potatoes and cook for 10 minutes until tender.

Meanwhile, add the milk to a large mixing bowl and microwave until hot (30 seconds), then add the salmon to the hot milk and microwave for another 30 seconds. Remove from the microwave, cover with a tea/dish towel and set aside. (Alternatively, warm the milk in a medium saucepan until just simmering, remove from the heat, add the salmon and cover.) This will let the salmon partially poach/steam in the milk.

Zest and halve the lemon. Finely chop the parsley, dill, cornichons and spring onions/scallions.

Once the potatoes are cooked, drain in a colander/strainer, then pop the colander on top of the (now empty) saucepan and leave to steam for 5 minutes. Remove the salmon from the milk (reserve the milk in the bowl) and place on top of the potatoes, so it will cook a little more from the residual heat.

GOES WELL WITH They're obviously great with Tartare Sauce (page 64), but also salsa verde.

LEFTOVERS They are wonderful reheated and eaten as they are (to reheat, place on a baking sheet, cover with foil and cook in an oven preheated to 180°C fan/200°C/400°F/Gas 6 for 15 minutes or until piping hot). Or break them up slightly with some extra mashed potato and make a kind of fishcake/bubble and squeak scenario, then pop a fried egg on top and some hot sauce. Yum!

Add the lemon zest, parsley, dill, cornichons and spring onions/scallions to the milk bowl along with the sumac and the juice of half the lemon. Once the potatoes and salmon have had their 5 minutes in the colander, add them to the milky mixing bowl. Very roughly mash the potatoes with the back of a spoon, also breaking up the salmon (but leave some chunks for texture), then mix all the ingredients together and make sure you season well – this is important.

Add the flour to a wide shallow bowl, the whisked egg to another and finally the breadcrumbs to a third bowl.

Using your hands, bring the salmon and potato mixture together and shape into 4 fishcakes.

Take one fishcake and dip it in the flour to lightly coat, pass it gently from one hand to another to get rid of any excess flour, then dip it into the egg wash, coat well and finally dip it in the breadcrumbs, making sure you generously coat the cakes. Transfer to a plate and repeat with the 3 other fishcakes.

Pour the oil into a large, non-stick frying pan/skillet set over a high heat. Once the oil is hot enough (drop a pinch of breadcrumbs in and if they immediately rise to the surface and gently sizzle, it's ready), add the fishcakes to the pan (I use a 22-cm/8¾-inch pan and cook 2 fishcakes at a time). Let them fry for 2–3 minutes on each side until crispy and golden brown, then serve immediately.

YELLOW FISH CURRY

I love a mild fish curry, nice and saucy, comforting and fragrant, which is exactly what this recipe offers. The flavours are obviously heavily inspired and influenced by a Thai yellow curry, but instead of creating an authentic curry paste first, I have just added those spices and aromatics to the pan. Whilst I'd advise you make this recipe with the intended white fish, I must say that it also works nicely as a veggie, chicken or pork curry. If they're the ingredients that need to be used up, then do a swap-in and try fish next time. Please note that meat will need longer cooking than the fish timings I've suggested here.

1 large onion	Any onion, shallot or leek
3 large garlic cloves	Purée or lazy garlic is fine here
60 g/2¼ oz. piece of fresh ginger	Purée is fine too
1 green chilli/chile	Any chilli/chile, dried chilli/hot red pepper flakes or a little powder
1 lemongrass	If you only have dried, use that, or omit
½ teaspoon ground turmeric	Omit if you don't have it
1 teaspoon mustard seeds	Any colour is fine
1 tablespoon curry powder	Any curry powder, but the most standard is best
1 teaspoon ground coriander	Crushed coriander seeds are great
1 star anise	A pinch of ground is fine, or just leave out
400-g/14-oz. can of coconut milk	Essential
2 tablespoons fish sauce	If you don't have it, just leave out
1 teaspoon honey	A pinch of sugar
100 g/2 cups spinach	Any light, leafy green or sliced spring onions/scallions
500 g/1 lb. 2 oz. sustainable white fish mix, in large chunks	Or just some sustainable haddock if you can't get a good mix
1 lime, into wedges	A little lemon would be ok instead of lime
coconut oil, for frying	
sea salt and freshly ground pepper	
jasmine rice, to serve	
fresh coriander/cilantro, to serve	
crispy onions (store bought), to serve	
SERVES 4	*TOTAL TIME 45 MINUTES*

Place a heaped dessertspoon of coconut oil in a large saucepan set over a medium heat. While it melts in the pan, halve, peel and thinly slice the onion. Once hot, add the onion and fry for 10 minutes, until softening and caramelized. Meanwhile, peel and finely slice the garlic. Trim the ginger and cut into matchsticks (no need to peel). Trim and finely slice the chilli/chile. Bash the lemongrass, then finely chop.

When the onions have had their time, add the garlic, ginger, chilli/chile and lemongrass, and fry for 2 minutes, until fragrant. Next, add the turmeric, mustard seeds, curry powder, ground coriander and star anise. Fry for a further 2 minutes, also until fragrant, then pour in the coconut milk, fish sauce and honey. Half-fill the coconut milk can with water and add that too.

Stir to combine the ingredients and bring to the boil. Once bubbling, reduce the temperature to a low simmer, and gently cook for 10 minutes. Taste to check for seasoning – you'll want to add a good pinch of sea salt, to even out the sweetness.

Add the spinach to the pan, mix well and let it wilt for a minute or so, then add the fish to the pan and poach for 5 minutes, until just cooked through and tender. Only stir the fish a couple of times, but no more than that (you don't want to break up the fish). Remove the pan from the heat, squeeze over some lime juice and taste to check for seasoning one last time.

Serve on jasmine rice, with a handful of torn coriander/cilantro, crispy onions and any spare lime wedges.

GOES WELL WITH Try the serving options above, but it is also lovely with a drizzle of my Coriander and Chilli Sauce (page 65).

LEFTOVERS I like to reheat this curry and toast some tortilla wraps to use as a scooping vessel instead of eating it with more rice. Or make some mashed potato for a curried fish pie. It also freezes well.

PORK & BEAN BURGERS

This recipe was one I originally created using some pork belly leftover from our wedding feast. It was the gift that kept on giving! I would say, however, that whilst using pork belly was delicious, the super high fat content of the meat meant that the mix had a particularly loose texture, so it was hard for the patties to remain stuck together. So, I've revised it to use pork mince/ground pork, which is a much more natural fit for a burger mix and allows the chipotle to really penetrate the meat.

BURGER BITS	
4 brioche buns	Pitta breads, flatbread, bread rolls, wraps, anything bready!
2 vine tomatoes	Any type of tomato
1 avocado	Thinly sliced cucumber or pickles
4 tablespoons mayonnaise	Sour cream or strained natural yogurt is great
2 tablespoons chipotle paste	Essential
Coriander and Chilli Sauce (page 65)	Any hot sauce is fine
20 g/¾ oz. rocket/arugula	Any lettuce will do
8 slices of cheese	I'm partial to Leerdamer or mozzarella
PORK PATTIES	
1 shallot, peeled	Any sort of onion
3 garlic cloves, peeled	Purée or lazy garlic
100 g/3½ oz. canned black beans, drained and rinsed	Kidney, haricot or borlotti/cranberry beans
500 g/1 lb. 2 oz. pork mince/ground pork	Beef or chicken mince, or a mixture – I love pork and beef mixed
2 tablespoons chipotle paste	Essential
sea salt and freshly ground pepper	
SERVES 4	**TOTAL TIME 40 MINUTES**

I like to have the 'building station' ready to go so that when the burgers are cooked, you can load up and inhale straight away, so...

Preheat the grill/broiler to its highest setting. Halve the brioche buns and place them all on a large baking sheet, then set aside. Gather all your 'burger bits', then thinly slice the tomatoes and avocado, mix the mayo and chipotle paste together with a pinch of seasoning (taste, then add more chipotle to your liking) and line up the Coriander and Chilli Sauce and rocket/arugula, too.

Now you can make the patties. Finely chop the shallot, then grate the garlic. Add them to a large mixing bowl with the beans, and roughly mash with a fork. Next, add the pork, chipotle paste and a very generous scattering of seasoning. Using your hands, mix the ingredients and

shape into 8 burger patties. Think American-style, thin and wide patties, as the buns will be loaded with 2 patties each. I tend to aim for 5 mm/¼ inch thick, 9 cm/3½ inches in diameter, or thereabouts.

Heat a drizzle of oil in a large, non-stick frying pan/skillet set over a high heat and once hot, add the patties (2 or 4, depending on the size of your pan) to the pan and fry for 2–3 minutes on each side, until browned and almost cooked through – treat them like a steak. Feel free to push down on them slightly with a spatula as they cook.

Whilst your burgers cook, pop the baking sheet of brioche buns under the preheated grill/broiler for 1–2 minutes to lightly brown, then remove and place the buns at your building station to get them out of the way.

You can now lay your cooked burger patties on that same baking sheet to. Once all the burgers are cooked, top them each with a slice of cheese and then pop back under the grill/broiler for 3 minutes. You want the cheese fully melted and bubbling away.

Load up the burger buns in whatever order you like with some chipotle mayo, fresh tomato and avocado slices, rocket/arugula, Coriander and Chilli Sauce, and of course the burgers themselves. Enjoy!

GOES WELL WITH These burgers have quite a lot going on, but the Lemon and Pecorino Polenta Fries (page 151) are great on the side.

LEFTOVERS Break up the leftover patties and fry them with some peanuts and spring onions/scallions, then using Little Gem/Boston lettuce as boats, load the lettuce leaves with re-fried burger meat, tomatoes, avocado and sauces, like a Mexican-style larb.

BUTTER BEAN SALAD WITH LAMB CHOPS

It's so satisfying to be able to whip up a refreshing salad with what's in the cupboard. Using up pantry items can feel like a winter task, but canned goods shouldn't be avoided just because it's getting warmer and there's fresh produce around. Here all you need is the lamb and some sort of fresh greenery, and the rest are store-cupboard or fridge staples.

LAMB & MARINADE	
4 lamb chops	Any sort of lamb, beef or pork steak cut, or boneless chicken thighs
1 tablespoon Dijon mustard	Grainy mustard, Greek or natural yogurt
2 tablespoons extra virgin olive oil	Any sort of oil, but olive oil is best
2 tablespoons sherry vinegar	Cider, red or white wine vinegar
8 sprigs of fresh rosemary	Fresh thyme, oregano, mint or marjoram
SALAD	
80 g/1½ cups fresh spinach	Any tender young leaf or lettuce – try rocket/arugula, Gem/Boston, pak choi/bok choy
2 x 400-g/14-oz. cans of butter/lima beans, drained and rinsed	Any cooked bean or legume – chickpeas work well
2 tablespoons capers, drained	Any sort of pickled vegetable, roughly chopped – cornichons are a good option
15 g/2 tablespoons pine nuts, toasted	Any nut or seed, toasted (and roughly chopped if larger than a pine nut)
SALAD DRESSING	
40 g/⅓ cup Greek yogurt	Natural yogurt, whole milk (half the quantity) or dairy-free yogurt
2 teaspoons honey	Maple, date or agave syrup or a brown sugar
2 teaspoons grainy mustard	Dijon or English mustard, or omit
freshly squeezed juice of 1 lemon	1 lime or a splash of vinegar (any type)
1 garlic clove, peeled and grated	Garlic purée, lazy chopped garlic (half the quantity with these) or omit
GREEN SAUCE	
20 g/¾ oz. fresh soft herbs	Anything soft, such as coriander/cilantro, parsley, chives, dill, basil, mint (but probably not sage)
120 ml/½ cup extra virgin olive oil	Any oil, but olive oil is best
30 g/1 oz. Parmesan	Pecorino, any hard Italian cheese or even feta
15 g/2 tablespoons pine nuts, toasted	As above
sea salt and freshly ground pepper	
SERVES 2	**TOTAL TIME 30 MINUTES**

GOES WELL WITH This is a great complete meal, but a tomato salad, some crispy potatoes or roasted baby carrots would work well on the side.

LEFTOVERS They're great in a pasta dish – chop up the meat and make a beany brothy sauce for the lamb and serve with some pasta or cooked grains.

Heat up the barbecue or use a large, non-stick frying pan/skillet set over a high heat.

Add the lamb chops to a bowl and top with all the marinade ingredients, along with a generous sprinkling of cracked black pepper. Work with your hands to combine and coat the meat, then set aside.

To prepare the salad, add the spinach, butter/lima beans, capers and pine nuts to a large salad bowl and set aside (you can toss later when you dress).

Next, add all the salad dressing ingredients to a jar, seal the lid and shake well to combine. Taste to check for seasoning and add a glug more oil and lemon juice if it needs loosening up.

For the green sauce, add the ingredients to a high-powered blender and blitz until very smooth. It may separate but that's ok. Taste and check for seasoning. It's meant to be lighter than a reduced sauce, but richer and oilier than a dressing.

Once the barbecue or frying pan/skillet is almost smoking hot (if using a pan, heat up with some rapeseed/canola oil over a high heat), remove the lamb from the marinade and season with sea salt, then place on the grill or in the pan. Pop the rosemary stalks from the marinade on top of the chops so the flavours continue to infuse. Fry (without touching or moving the chops) for 3–4 minutes on each side, until wonderfully charred, caramelized and tender. This timing will cook the meat to medium; if you prefer your lamb well-done, just cook for another couple of minutes on each side, then transfer to a plate to rest.

Pour the salad dressing on top of the beans and spinach, toss to coat and pile onto serving plates, add the rested chops and finish by drizzling over the green sauce.

GOES WELL WITH Marinated Feta (page 29) or barbecued meat. I love it with a roast chicken, too.

LEFTOVERS Stuff it into a wrap with grilled chicken or steak. Or add more herbs, fresh salad and top with feta to make it into a second salad.

MIXED BEAN SALAD

Mixed bean salads are such a good side dish when you need to bulk out a spread with either not much time or not much produce. Grab a couple of cans and you're halfway there. My aunt, Wendy is the queen of rustling up a wicked bean salad, different every time and always full of random store-cupboard gems. I've thickened this one up with some nutty red rice and boiled eggs, all brought together with a great miso dressing. I hope you like it.

SALAD	
2 eggs, at room temperature	Could be omitted if necessary
100 g/½ cup red rice	Wholegrain rice or just plain basmati
¼ red onion	A couple of sliced pickles
5 g/¼ oz. fresh dill	Parsley or coriander/cilantro are best, but basil or mint could work too
2 x 400-g/14-oz. cans of beans – best to have a mixture	Try cannellini, butter/lima, haricot, black, kidney, borlotti/cranberry or flageolet
DRESSING	
1 tablespoon white miso	Red miso can be used
freshly squeezed juice of 1 lemon	Lime is fine here, or a dash of white wine vinegar
1 teaspoon honey	Agave, or some golden caster/granulated sugar
3 tablespoons extra virgin olive oil	Normal olive oil or sesame oil would be lovely too
sea salt and freshly ground pepper	
SERVES 4–6	*TOTAL TIME 1 HOUR*

Bring a saucepan of water to the boil, then add the eggs. Boil for 8 minutes, then scoop them out of the water (save the pan of water) and immediately plunge the eggs into cold water. Once cool enough to handle, peel. Leave them whole until later.

Pour the rice directly into the pan of boiling water that was used for the eggs, bring back to the boil and cook according to packet instructions (probably about 45 minutes for red rice).

While the rice cooks, peel and very thinly slice the red onion, roughly chop the fresh dill, drain and rinse the beans. Add them all to a salad bowl and aside (it's best not to mix up yet).

Add all the dressing ingredients to a small bowl and whisk well with a fork. Taste to check for seasoning and set aside. So, you should have a salad bowl with beans, dill and onion in, then separately, the dressing and the peeled, cold eggs, all patiently waiting.

Once the rice is ready, drain in a sieve/strainer, placing it under cold running water to cool, then add to the salad bowl. Pour in all the dressing, add a good pinch of seasoning and toss to combine. Slice the eggs into wedges and pop them on the top, then serve immediately, or store in the fridge until needed. If refrigerated, let the salad sit at room temperature for 30 minutes before serving, so it's not too cold.

ROASTED CANNED ARTICHOKES WITH LEMON & SMOKED SALT

These are my go-to nibbles if friends suddenly turn up at the front door with a bottle and I've got nothing in the fridge to serve. They couldn't be simpler (and cheaper), especially as canned artichokes and an old lemon are often to be found lurking in my kitchen.

2 x 400-g/14-oz. cans of artichokes, drained	Raw green beans, Tenderstem broccoli/broccolini or courgette/zucchini batons
3 tablespoons olive oil	Vegetable, rapeseed/canola, sunflower oil or sesame oil
zest and freshly squeezed juice of 1 lemon, plus extra lemon wedges to serve	1 lime, bottled lemon juice or a dash of vinegar
½ tablespoon smoked sea salt	Sea salt, table salt (if it's fine salt, use less)
60 g/¼ cup mayonnaise	Plain, Greek or dairy-free yogurt
SERVES 4 AS A SNACK	**TOTAL TIME 30 MINUTES**

Preheat the oven to 220°C fan/240°C/450°F/Gas 8.

Halve the artichoke hearts, place on a large baking sheet and then drizzle over the oil, squeeze the juice of half a lemon on top and toss to coat. Scatter the smoked sea salt over and roast on the top shelf of the preheated oven for 30 minutes, turning half way through cooking.

Meanwhile, mix the remaining lemon juice with the mayo, lemon zest and a pinch of seasoning.

The artichokes are done when they golden brown, crispy and brittle at the edges. Serve them with the lemony mayo, more smoked salt and lemon wedges.

GOES WELL WITH A glass of Riesling!

LEFTOVERS Fold into a risotto or fresh pasta, serve on toast with some ricotta or toss through a crunchy salad.

GOES WELL WITH Whatever you like!
I enjoy yogurt, banana and date syrup
with these pancakes.

LEFTOVERS Pancakes are really yummy
broken up, re-fried in butter until crisp
and sprinkled on top of ice cream, as a
make-shift dessert. Or add into a bread
and butter pudding.

PORRIDGE & NUT BUTTER PANCAKES

I always have leftover porridge – is it possible to make the right amount? I freeze any surplus and defrost it for weekend pancakes. It bulks out the batter and makes for a delicious pancake, giving it a more robust, yet still fluffy texture. I use a mix of nut butters, whether it be almond, peanut, cashew or even Nutella (if using this, you won't need to add the honey).

200 g/7 oz. leftover porridge	Essential
100 g/7 tablespoons nut butter	Any nut butter: peanut, almond, cashew, Nutella
1 egg, beaten	Use 50 g/2 oz. banana or yogurt
2 tablespoons runny honey	Agave, date syrup, maple syrup, sugar of any kind
100 ml/⅓ cup plus 1 tablespoon whole milk	Any milk, including dairy-free, oat or almond
100 g/¾ cup self-raising/rising flour	Any flour but if there's no raising agent, double the quantity of baking powder
1 teaspoon baking powder	Can be omitted
¼ teaspoon sea salt	Can be omitted
butter, for frying	
MAKES 10 PANCAKES	**TOTAL TIME 30 MINUTES**

Preheat the oven to 100°C fan/120°C/250°F/Gas ½.

Add the porridge and nut butter to a large mixing bowl and mix vigorously with a fork, to break up and combine the two chunky ingredients. Don't worry if there are lumps of nut butter, but try to break up the porridge. Add the egg, honey and half the milk to the bowl, then whisk once more, fully incorporating all the ingredients together.

You're often told to add the wet ingredients to the dry, but for this recipe I just chuck the 'dry' on top of the 'wet' for ease. So, add the flour (sift it in if you can be bothered, I never do), baking powder and salt on top of the wet mix and fold into each other using a spatula, gradually adding the remaining milk as you do so. Try not to overmix; get them all combined, but the briefer the better.

Add a knob/pat of butter to a non-stick frying pan/skillet, and once melted and gently sizzling, add 2 heaped dessert spoons of mixture on top of one another to create your first pancake. Depending on the size of your pan, scoop in another pancake, and a third if there's space.

Let them gently fry for 2–3 minutes on one side until you see bubbles form on the surface, then flip over and fry for the same amount of time on the other side. You can check underneath when you think they're done, and you should find a nice golden-brown crust.

Transfer to an ovenproof dish to keep warm, then repeat the process with the remaining batter. Make sure you add another knob/pat of butter to the pan as needed. Once they're all ready, serve with whatever toppings you like (see my suggestions for inspiration).

WAWA'S TIFFIN

This is not actually from Wawa (my maternal grandmother) – it came from her friend Moira, known as Auntie Moira to my mother. We found it in Wawa's homemade cookbook and it is so good. My sisters have loved making it over the last few years and I've been happily swung over to Auntie Moira's ways. She includes an egg, which isn't that usual for a tiffin, but it really adds to the rich decadence of this fridge treat. I tend to do just a thin layer of dark chocolate on top, as the tiffin itself is very sweet, but add more by all means.

250 g/9 oz. digestive biscuits/graham crackers	Any biscuit/cookie (I think Hobnobs are a delicious replacement)
100 g/¾ cup raisins	Any dried fruit, go wild! A mixture is also welcome
110 g/scant ½ cup unsalted butter	Essential, salted is fine if it's all you have
50 g/heaping ⅓ cup icing/ confectioner's sugar	Caster/granulated sugar, but you need to make sure it dissolves in the pan
2 tablespoons cocoa powder	Essential
1 egg, whisked	Essential, according to Auntie Moira
100 g/3½ oz. dark/bittersweet chocolate	Any chocolate (use milk or white if you prefer, but I think dark/bittersweet is best)
½ teaspoon sea salt	Not essential, but very delicious
SERVES 8–12	**TOTAL TIME 20 MINUTES, PLUS SETTING**

23-cm/9-inch square baking pan lined with parchment paper

Break up the biscuits/crackers well by either placing them in a freezer bag and bashing them with a rolling pin or pulsing them a few times in a food processor. Transfer them to a large mixing bowl, along with the raisins.

Add the butter, sugar and cocoa powder to a saucepan and gently melt over a low heat for 3–5 minutes until fully melted, mixing often. Once it's a nice, loose mix, remove from the heat and whisk the egg in quickly and thoroughly. It might look a little lumpy for a minute, but keep whisking and it'll smooth out and thicken slightly. Pour the butter mix over the biscuits and stir very well to combine and fully coat.

Pile the tiffin mix into the prepared baking pan and press down well with the back of the spatula or wooden spoon to create a compact tiffin with a level top.

Melt the chocolate in a bain marie (or microwave in 30-second bursts, stirring in between each burst), then pour on top of the tiffin. Once all the chocolate has been poured, lift the baking pan and tilt gently from side to side to encourage the chocolate to spread over the entire surface of the tiffin. Sprinkle the salt on top and transfer to the fridge for 30 minutes to set. Slice it up and enjoy!

GOES WELL WITH A cup of tea.

LEFTOVERS They live in the fridge and are best consumed at absolutely any time that you would like one.

SUMMER

TOMATO & SESAME SALAD

This is a super simple, fresh tomato salad but with the addition of sesame (both seeds and oil) because I think they go so well together. It's half fresh, half store-cupboard items. I haven't been very generous with swap-in ingredients, but this is the sort of recipe that you are going to make when you have a bowl of ripe tomatoes so I think you'll be ok.

10 g/1 tablespoon sesame seeds	Essential
600 g/1 lb. 5 oz. ripe mixed tomatoes	Essential
20 g/¾ oz. fresh basil	You could use any soft herbs. Mint is heaven, too
2 tablespoons extra virgin olive oil	Normal olive oil is fine, but not as good
50 ml/3½ tablespoons sesame oil	Essential
2 tablespoons sherry vinegar	Red wine vinegar or apple cider vinegar
sea salt and freshly ground pepper	
SERVES 4–6 AS A SIDE	*TOTAL TIME 10 MINUTES*

Add the sesame seeds to a frying pan/skillet and place over a low-medium heat. Let the pan come up to temperature and then let the seeds toast for a couple of minutes, tossing often to avoid any burning. Once golden, remove from the heat.

Roughly slice, wedge or halve the tomatoes, however you like. Remove the basil leaves from their stalks and finely slice the stalks (keep the leaves whole).

Transfer the tomatoes and basil to a salad bowl and add the toasted sesame seeds, oils and vinegar, along with a pinch of seasoning, tossing everything together to coat and combine. Leave on the side for 30 minutes (or even longer if you have time) before serving.

GOES WELL WITH Wonky Stuffed Flatbreads (page 42) to scoop up the salad and soak up the dressing juices, or add some crackers, cured meat and Marinated Feta (page 29) for a summer mezze.

LEFTOVERS I love the leftovers, just make sure you bring them out of the fridge in good time so they're not cold when you enjoy this salad again. It's lovely with some cooked pasta and rocket/arugula folded through, or boiled rice for that matter.

GREENS ON TOAST

This recipe can use whatever greens you have, whether they be fresh or frozen, sturdy or limping. Just get them in a pan with some lemon and chilli/chile and you're good to go. It's also great with an egg on top, if you so wish. Very, very simple, super quick and one of my favourite lunches when working at home. Best eaten with the sun on your face if possible.

200 g/7 oz. greens	Spinach, broccoli, cabbage, pak choi/bok choi, edamame, peas, broad/fava beans, French beans, sugar snaps, mangetout, kale, cavolo nero, chard, beetroot/beet leaves, radish tops, rocket/arugula, endive, watercress, spring greens… A mix is fine – I like to use 150 g/5½ oz. leafy greens and top up with 50 g/2 oz. spinach
2 large slices of bread	Any bread is fine
a pinch (or two) of dried chilli/hot red pepper flakes	A pinch of cayenne pepper or a dash of chilli/chili oil
1 lemon	Fresh lime juice or a dash of white wine vinegar
butter, for frying	
extra virgin olive oil, for drizzling	
SERVES 2	**TOTAL TIME 10 MINUTES**

Roughly slice the greens if they need it, but leave delicate/smaller leaves whole (spinach, rocket/arugula, beetroot/beet tops). Add a good knob/pat of butter to a large frying pan/skillet set over a medium heat. Pop the bread in the toaster (or under the grill/broiler).

Once the butter is sizzling, add the greens with a good pinch of seasoning and chilli/hot red pepper flakes and fry for 3–5 minutes until wilted and fairly tender, but still vibrant, green and with a bite. Add a good squeeze of lemon juice and remove from the heat.

If your greens are light and leafy, they'll only take a minute or two in the pan, so if using a mixture, add the thicker or hardier ones first (broccoli, beans, thick cabbage, mangetout etc) and give them 3–5 minutes in the pan, then add the leafy greens (spinach, kale, cavolo nero, rocket/arugula, peas etc) for a minute or two at the end, just to wilt and tenderize.

Put the toast on a serving plate and pile on the buttery, lemony greens, drizzling any pan butter over. Finish with a drizzle of olive oil and an extra pinch of chilli/hot red pepper flakes if you like. Serve immediately.

GOES WELL WITH Marinated Feta (page 29) or Labneh (page 33), which are both great spread on the toast before the greens are popped on top.

LEFTOVERS Fold through some noodles – you could add them to the Tofu Noodles with Mushrooms and Marmite (page 77) – or reheat and serve with freshly cooked fish.

HERB, HAZELNUT & ASPARAGUS PASTA

In the summer, always cook more pasta than you need for a meal as a pasta salad is delicious, cheap, very quick to rustle up from leftovers and great for using up surplus veg. I've used glorious asparagus here, but it lends itself very well to plenty of seasonal greens.

250 g/9 oz. asparagus	Courgette/zucchini, cut into thin strips
40 g/⅓ cup hazelnuts	Any nuts – almonds and walnuts are lovely
50 g/⅓ cup pine nuts	Any nuts, especially almonds, walnuts, chopped Brazil nuts
240 g/8½ oz. dried pasta	Any sort of pasta; my favourite is linguine or tagliatelle
20 g/¾ oz. Parmesan	Any hard cheese, but an Italian hard cheese is best
4 tablespoons extra virgin olive oil	Olive oil, walnut oil, cold pressed rapeseed/canola oil
1 lemon	Essential
15 g/½ oz. fresh soft herbs (basil, parsley, chives, dill)	Any fresh herbs, and/or some crunchy salad leaves
sea salt and freshly ground pepper	

SERVES 4 | **TOTAL TIME 25 MINUTES**

Preheat the oven to 200°C fan/220°C/425°F/Gas 7. Bring a large pan of salted water to the boil.

Break off the ends of the asparagus stalks by holding them at each end and gently bending – they'll naturally break at the perfect point (pop the hardy ends in the freezer and add to your next stock). Halve the asparagus stalks lengthways and place them on a baking sheet.

Roughly chop the hazelnuts and place on the baking sheet with the asparagus and pine nuts. Drizzle a generous glug of olive oil over the nuts and veg, seasoning well too, then place on the top shelf of the hot oven for 10 minutes, until golden and tenderizing.

Once the water is boiling, add the pasta to the pan and cook according to packet instructions (for dried, it's usually 9–11 minutes). Drain, and rinse under cold water until fully cooled, then set aside, with a little drizzle of olive oil folded through to avoid it sticking together.

Grate the Parmesan into a large salad bowl, add the extra virgin olive oil, lemon zest and juice, and a pinch of seasoning, then whisk with a fork to combine. Tear the herbs (and their stalks) into the bowl. Pile in the pasta when it's drained and ready, then add the warm, roasted asparagus and nuts. Add some extra seasoning and toss very thoroughly, then serve.

GOES WELL WITH Really nice as a stand-alone lunch, but the Tomato and Sesame Salad (page 100) is great alongside.

LEFTOVERS Lasts in the fridge for a couple of days, just make sure you take it out of the fridge 30 minutes before you re-serve. It might need a fresh glug of oil and lemon juice. Pile in some fresh salad leaves and a scattering of extra Parmesan, if you like.

CHIPOTLE RED PEPPER SOUP

While this is a fantastic summer soup, it can also be made all year round. On hot days I love this soup fridge cold, like a Spanish gazpacho – serve it with an ice cube and some fresh mint, along with the basil. Add an extra pinch of salt and pepper – when things are cold, their flavours are slightly muted, so it can take an extra hit of seasoning at the end.

4 red (bell) peppers	Essential
2 large brown onions	Any type of onion, shallot or spring onion/scallion
3 garlic cloves	Chopped, purée or powder (use 1 teaspoon)
350 g/12 oz. tomatoes	Any ripe tomatoes or 400-g/14-oz. can of tomatoes
1 tablespoon smoked paprika	Sweet paprika is fine or omit
1 teaspoon ground coriander	Ground cumin or crushed whole coriander seeds
1 tablespoon chipotle paste	Essential
400 ml/1¾ cups vegetable stock	Chicken stock, or just water
1 teaspoon light brown muscovado sugar	Any type of brown sugar or honey, or even white sugar
10 g/⅓ oz. fresh basil	Parsley, chives, coriander/cilantro, dill
2 tablespoons extra virgin olive oil	Olive oil or a nut oil
olive oil, for roasting	
butter, for frying	
sea salt and freshly ground pepper	
SERVES 4	*TOTAL TIME 45 MINUTES*

Preheat the oven to 220°C fan/240°C/450°F/Gas 8.

Discard the (bell) pepper stalk (leave the pith and seeds) and chop into 3–4-cm/1¼–1½-inch pieces. Add to a large baking sheet, drizzle with olive oil, season generously and toss to coat. Place on the top shelf of the oven and roast for 20 minutes, until tender and lightly charred.

Meanwhile, halve and thinly slice the onions. Melt a knob/pat of butter in a large casserole dish/Dutch oven or saucepan. When gently sizzling, add the onion. Gently fry for 15 minutes, until soft and lightly caramelized. Peel and thinly slice the garlic. Roughly chop the tomatoes. Add the garlic, spices and chipotle paste to the pan and fry for 2 minutes, until fragrant. Add the tomatoes, stock, sugar and the roasted veg (if they're not ready, just add them later).

Bring to the boil, then reduce the heat to a very gentle simmer and cook for 10 minutes. Remove the pan from the heat, then blitz the soup using a stick/immersion blender. Taste to check for seasoning and add more salt, pepper and chipotle paste to your liking. Divide into bowls, scatter over fresh basil and add a drizzle of extra virgin olive oil. Serve immediately.

GOES WELL WITH Breadcrumbs (page 37) and Hunk of Cheese Scones (page 26).

LEFTOVERS Makes a great (and super quick) Romesco sauce (page 145).

WHOLE BAKED FENNEL

I love fennel – raw, roasted, barbecued, braised, however it comes. This is a nice, simple, stick-it-in-the-oven recipe that can be a bold side dish or stand-alone meal accompanied by a fresh salad. It's got great, confident ingredients, so be ready for a punchy (almost) veggie dish. You can remove the anchovies if you want it to become veggie/vegan, but if you do, add some capers to help with that savoury hit you're losing.

1 vine tomato	Any fresh or sun-dried/sun-blush tomatoes
3 large garlic cloves	Essential
5 g/¼ oz. fresh oregano	Thyme, parsley or basil
1 lemon	Essential
2 whole fennel bulbs	Essential
3 anchovy fillets	1 tablespoon capers, caperberries or pitted olives
2 tablespoons olive oil	Any oil
1 tablespoon red wine vinegar	Sherry vinegar, white wine vinegar or cider vinegar
Parmesan, to serve (optional)	Any hard Italian cheese
sea salt and freshly ground pepper	
SERVES 2–4	*TOTAL TIME 1 HOUR 40 MINUTES*

Preheat the oven to 180°C fan/200°C/400°F/Gas 6.

Thinly slice the tomato, then peel and thinly slice the garlic. Remove the oregano leaves from the stalks and cut the lemon into wedges.

Stand a fennel bulb upright, so it's sitting on its base, then cut a cross down into its heart, without cutting all the way through. Repeat with the second bulb and place on a baking sheet lined with parchment paper. Keep the fennel upright and then stuff with the prepared tomato slices, anchovies (use whole or tear up to spread them out), garlic and oregano. Generously fill the crevices of the fennel bulbs, both the ones made with the knife and the naturally occurring ones as the layers separate towards the tip of the bulbs – this doesn't need to be done neatly!

Drizzle a good glug of olive oil over the stuffed fennel, along with the vinegar and a squeeze of lemon juice too. Season well, then lay the stuffed bulbs on their side, making sure you add the lemon wedges to the tray. Give them one final drizzle of oil over the top, too.

Place on the top shelf of the preheated oven and roast for 45 minutes, until caramelized, tender and smelling divine, but not quite ready. Baste the fennel with the pan juices, then return to the oven for another 45 minutes. Keep an eye on them in the oven and if you're worried about burning, cover them, although I like the charred bits so I rarely do.

Once ready, serve the baked fennel sprinkled with a little grated Parmesan, if you like.

GOES WELL WITH Barbecued meat
or fish and my Tomato and Sesame
Salad (page 100) are a lovely
combination. I don't think you
need much else for a great
weekend feast.

LEFTOVERS Slice up and make
into a delicious pasta sauce, with
some extra tomatoes and a
generous spoonful of mascarpone
or crème fraîche.

PRAWN & ONION PIL PIL

This gorgeous summery recipe is, of course, fully inspired by and an ode to the Spanish pil pil that so many of us adore. I am in love with this recipe. The shallots are crispy, yet chewy, stringy, but also gooey, and when paired with the sweet prawns/shrimp and smoky, warming oil... it's a joy.

1 crunchy white baguette	Any bread, but something that can soak up oil!
1 shallot	An onion of any colour
6 garlic cloves	Essential
20 raw prawns/shrimp	Essential
5 g/¼ oz. fresh parsley	Can be omitted, but I like the freshness
200 ml/¾ cup olive oil	Essential
a generous pinch of dried chilli/hot red pepper flakes	A small pinch of chilli/chili powder
½ teaspoon smoked paprika	Ideal, but can be omitted
sea salt and freshly ground pepper	
SERVES 2 AS A SHARING STARTER/ LUNCH	*TOTAL TIME 15 MINUTES*

Preheat the oven to 150°C fan/170°C/325°F/Gas 3, then pop the baguette in the oven to warm up while you make the dish.

Peel, halve and thinly slice the shallot lengthways. Peel and slice the garlic. De-shell and de-vein the prawns/shrimp, seasoning them too. Finely chop the fresh parsley and set aside.

Add the oil to a medium frying pan/skillet (I use one with a 26-cm/10¼-inch diameter), along with the shallot, chilli/hot red pepper flakes and smoked paprika and set over a medium heat. Once the shallot and chilli flakes start sizzling, leave them for 2 minutes, then add the garlic to the pan and fry for another 4 minutes.

Add the prawns, nestle them in and fry for a minute. Then turn the prawns over, remove the pan from the heat and let them continue to cook in the residual heat for a final minute. Season one final time and take the pan to the table or transfer to a serving bowl.

Sprinkle some parsley over the top and scoop up the prawns along with the sticky, crispy shallots with plenty of bread.

GOES WELL WITH A crisp white wine!

LEFTOVERS Great piled into a sandwich with some garlic mayo and Little Gem/Boston lettuce, or maybe turn them into a taco filling, served with a tomato salsa, guacamole, sour cream and some fresh chilli/chile.

FRUIT & COCONUT SPATCHCOCK CHICKEN

This is a winner which I first made for an impromptu family lunch. I had a whole chicken but not much else, apart from canned fruit and coconut milk. I whizzed up this marinade and served the chicken with brown rice and cucumber salad. Cook in the oven or on the barbecue.

400-g/14-oz. can of fruit	Pineapple, mango, peach, or a combination
1 chilli/chile	Any chilli/chile, dash of chilli powder or 1 teaspoon chilli/hot red pepper flakes
6 garlic cloves	Garlic is essential, but purée or powder is fine
25-g/1-oz. piece of fresh ginger	Add more garlic or use ginger purée
2 tablespoons soy sauce	Tamari, Worcestershire sauce or fish sauce
400-g/14-oz. can of coconut milk	You need this really, but cow's or almond milk will do
1 tablespoon ground coriander	Not a direct replacement but Cajun spice works well
2 tablespoons sesame oil	Any nut oil or olive oil
1 whole chicken	Essential, but bone-in thighs work well
sea salt and freshly ground pepper	
SERVES 4	*TOTAL TIME 45 MINUTES BARBECUE/1 HOUR OVEN*

Drain the canned fruit and trim the chilli/chile. Peel the garlic cloves. Roughly chop the ginger (no need to peel). Add all the ingredients (apart from the chicken, obviously) to a food processor, add a generous pinch of seasoning and blitz until smooth. This will make double the amount of marinade you need, so freeze half and save it for another day.

Place the chicken in a large roasting pan, then cut either side of the bird's spine using some strong scissors and remove the spine completely. Turn the chicken over and flatten by pushing down on the breasts, making sure the legs have been turned out and the thighs are facing up.

Pour half the marinade over the chicken, making sure you slather some on the underside too, and season again. Transfer to the fridge to marinate for a few hours, or even better overnight (it will still be great if you cook it straight away, so don't worry if time is of the essence).

Heat the barbecue to high. Once hot, put the chicken on the barbecue, breast side down. Let it cook for about 15–20 minutes until the skin is nicely charred, then turn it over and give it another 10 minutes, until fully cooked through (make sure you check – if you cut into the flesh the juices should run clear). Remove, let rest for 15 minutes, then carve and serve.

If using the oven, preheat the oven to 200°C fan/220°C/425°F/Gas 7. Roast (breasts up) for about 35 minutes, baste, then another 10 minutes. If you want the skin more charred, turn the grill/broiler on for 5 minutes at the end.

GOES WELL WITH Brown rice and a smacked cucumber salad.

LEFTOVERS Perfect, just perfect for Chicken, Mango and Cucumber Ciabatta (page 115).

CHICKEN, MANGO & CUCUMBER CIABATTA

I love most sandwiches, but this one really sings of summer. I made it the day after I'd cooked the Fruit and Coconut Spatchcock Chicken (page 112) and I also had a lovely ripe mango just waiting to be used. Alternatively, you can use leftover chicken from the Roast Chicken and Cider Stew (see page 138) and use mango chutney instead of the fresh mango – that way it can be enjoyed all year round!

1 ciabatta	Any type of bread or roll
130–150 g/4½–5½ oz. leftover cooked chicken	Any cooked chicken or pork, or fried halloumi
70 g/2½ oz. cucumber	Raw courgette/zucchini or fresh tomatoes
60 g/2 oz. fresh mango (or chutney)	Thinly sliced pineapple (fresh or canned), canned mango
60 g/4 tablespoons natural yogurt	Any yogurt or mayonnaise
10 g/⅓ oz. fresh mint	Basil or parsley, or more coriander/cilantro
10 g/⅓ oz. fresh coriander/cilantro	Basil, parsley, more mint, or omit
sea salt and freshly ground pepper	
SERVES 2	**TOTAL TIME 10 MINUTES**

Preheat the oven to 180°C fan/200°C/400°F/Gas 6. Once hot, pop the ciabattas in the oven to warm up for 5 minutes.

Prepare all of your ingredients by slicing the chicken, thinly slicing the cucumber, peeling and slicing the mango and seasoning the yogurt. Remove the mint leaves from their stalks (pop the stalks in a jug/pitcher of water to give you flavoured water). Leave the coriander/cilantro whole.

When the ciabattas are warm, cut through the centre and start loading up, in whatever order you like. Serve immediately and enjoy.

GOES WELL WITH The Lemon and Pecorino Polenta Fries (page 151) and some Coriander and Chilli Sauce too (page 65).

LEFTOVERS This is already a leftover recipe, but it works wonderfully in wraps or try all of these ingredients stirred through some cool noodles, too.

HERBY PEANUT VERMICELLI SALAD

This recipe is a great one for using up almost any herbs you've got in the fridge, teamed with a handful of store-cupboard items. It is also a great dish for adding leftover rare beef too as well, or chicken for that matter, so maybe a summery Monday evening, post-roast or barbecue, is a good time for this creation.

200 g/7 oz. vermicelli noodles	Any pre-made noodles
20 g/¾ oz. fresh soft herbs	Mint, Thai basil, chives, coriander/cilantro, parsley, basil
2 teaspoons chilli/chili oil	Olive oil and some chilli/hot red pepper flakes is fine
2 tablespoons sesame oil	Walnut oil will do, or rapeseed/canola oil
2 limes	Lemon juice, or an extra 1 teaspoon rice vinegar
2 tablespoons fish sauce	Can be omitted
40 g/3 tablespoons peanut butter	Any nut butter
2 teaspoons rice vinegar	White wine vinegar or black rice vinegar
60 g/⅔ cup salted peanuts	Any salted nut, but salted cashews probably best
SERVES 2	*TOTAL TIME 15 MINUTES*

Cook the vermicelli noodles according to packet instructions (I usually boil them for 3–4 minutes), then drain and rinse under cold water.

Tear up or roughly chop all the fresh soft herbs, including the stalks if they're not too hardy.

Add the oils, juice from both limes, fish sauce, peanut butter and rice vinegar to the base of a salad bowl and whisk vigorously to combine. Add in the vermicelli noodles, herbs and peanuts and toss to combine and coat. Serve immediately.

GOES WELL WITH Either leftover Bavette Steak (page 145) or leftover Fruit and Coconut Spatchcock Chicken (page 112).

LEFTOVERS Get some summer roll wrappers and use the noodles as filling along with some freshly chopped veg and cooked prawns/shrimp.

GOES WELL WITH A napkin!

LEFTOVERS There won't be
any, I promise you that.

BREADED CORN ON THE COB

Corn on the cob has got to be one of the most tasty and humbling dishes out there – no matter where you're from or how old you are, the best way to eat it is with your hands and you will get salty butter on your cheeks. This recipe turns the corn into a showstopper.

2 corn on the cob	Essential
1 lime	Lemon, or it's fine to leave it out
15 g/1 tablespoon white miso paste	Red miso, or try a combination of tahini and soy sauce
20 g/1½ tablespoons mayonnaise	Yogurt, cream cheese, sour cream, labneh (page 33)
50 g/1 cup breadcrumbs (if frozen, defrosted)	Essential, use panko if needed
10 g/1½ tablespoons finely grated Parmesan	Any strong, hard cheese
5 sprigs of fresh thyme	Fresh parsley, chives or dried thyme
½ teaspoon chilli/chili oil	A dash of olive oil and dried chilli/hot red pepper flakes
1 tablespoon sesame oil	Olive oil, rapeseed/canola oil, walnut oil
5 g/1 tablespoon freshly chopped coriander/cilantro	Fresh parsley, chives, chopped rocket/arugula, crispy onions
sea salt and freshly ground pepper	
SERVES 2	*TOTAL TIME 15 MINUTES*

Preheat the grill/broiler to high.

Bring a large pan of water to the boil and once boiling, pop the corn in and cook for 5 minutes until tender. Immediately remove the corn from the boiling water and rinse under cold water to cool down and stop the cooking process.

While the corn cooks, zest the lime into a small bowl and add the white miso, mayonnaise and a pinch of seasoning. Stir to fully combine. On a plate, mix the breadcrumbs, Parmesan, fresh thyme leaves (discard the stalks), chilli/chili oil and sesame oil with a pinch of sea salt and plenty of black pepper. Mix well to combine, then jiggle the plate to even out.

Once the corn is cool, dab dry with a clean tea/dish towel and place on a baking sheet lined with foil. Spread the miso mayo over the corn using the back of a teaspoon so the whole corn is covered, apart from the base on which it sits. Next, roll each corn cob in the breadcrumb mix, patting the crumb on, then place back on the baking sheet. Tip over any remaining breadcrumbs and gently pat them to secure, too. Pop under the preheated grill/broiler (or place on the top shelf of the oven) and grill/broil for 5–6 minutes until golden brown and smelling amazing.

Serve with freshly chopped coriander/cilantro on top and a squeeze of lime juice.

ROASTED MARROW & COURGETTE PASTA

Even if you don't have your own vegetable patch, you probably know someone who has one and ends up with a glut of marrow every year! One of my favourite ways to use it is this simple, creamy pasta sauce. You need to have tender, pre-roasted marrow before you start.

200 g/7 oz. dried pasta	Any type, fresh obviously fab too
1 onion	Any onion or shallot, fennel or celery
1 courgette/zucchini	Little Gem/Boston lettuce, or more marrow
150 g/5½ oz. pre-roasted marrow	Essential, or use more courgette/zucchini
1 teaspoon garlic purée	Fresh garlic, or ½ teaspoon garlic powder
100 ml whole milk	Any type of milk, dairy-free is fine
1 teaspoon Dijon mustard	Grainy or English is fine
1 lemon	A dash of white wine, or cider vinegar
grated Pecorino, to serve	Any hard cheese that can be grated is fine
olive oil, for frying	
sea salt and freshly ground pepper	
SERVES 2	*TOTAL TIME 35 MINUTES*

Fill a large saucepan with water and season very well. Bring to the boil, then add the pasta and cook according to packet instructions.

Add a glug of olive oil to a large, non-stick frying pan/skillet set over a medium heat. Halve, peel and thinly slice the onion and add to the pan, letting it sizzle for 15 minutes, gently frying and caramelizing. Stir often to avoid burning.

Meanwhile, halve the courgette/zucchini (no need to trim it) and thinly slice at an angle, then roughly chop the roasted marrow.

When the onions have had their 15 minutes, add the courgette and fry for 3 minutes, stirring often. Next, add the marrow and garlic and fry for another 2 minutes. Add the milk and mustard to the pan and let bubble for about 3 minutes, stirring almost constantly, until you have a gloopy, lumpy, sloppy but delicious sauce in the pan. Squeeze in half the lemon juice and taste to check for seasoning. Remove the sauce from the heat if the pasta is still cooking.

When the pasta is ready, reserve a mug of pasta cooking water, then drain. Tip the pasta into the sauce and pour in a splash of pasta water too. Put back on the heat and bring to a gentle simmer, stir or toss to combine well. If you think it's looking a bit dry, add a splash more pasta water. Taste to check for seasoning and add more lemon juice, salt and pepper to your taste. Pile into bowls and top with some Pecorino, then add a final drizzle of olive oil before serving.

GOES WELL WITH Just a lovely fresh salad, or the Tomato and Sesame Salad (page 100).

LEFTOVERS Make into a pasta bake. Add a little more milk to the leftovers to loosen up, then top with breadcrumbs, soft herbs and grated cheese (mix them up) and bake in a hot oven.

GARDEN SORBET

I love this recipe. Lots of fresh mint, lemon, apple and thyme are all combined to make this refreshing tangy sorbet. It's super simple, too, and you don't need an ice cream churner – phew! You do need fresh herbs, but the rest of the ingredients are pretty much staples.

30 g/1 oz. fresh mint	Essential
10 g/½ oz. fresh thyme	Lemon thyme works well, or add a bit more mint
280 ml/scant 1¼ cups water	
200 g/1 cup caster/granulated sugar	You need the sugar for this recipe, golden caster/granulated sugar is fine
130 ml/½ cup plus 2 teaspoons freshly squeezed lemon juice (about 4 lemons)	Lime or orange juice would be lovely, but please use fresh
150 ml/⅔ cup apple juice	Elderflower cordial (diluted with water) is a good swap
SERVES 6–8	*TOTAL TIME 15 MINUTES, THEN CHILLING AND OVERNIGHT FREEZING*

Add the mint, thyme, water and sugar to a small saucepan and bring to the boil over a low heat, so that the sugar can fully dissolve – this will take about 10 minutes. Once bubbling, reduce the heat slightly and let the mixture simmer for 2 minutes. Remove from the heat and let fully cool. If you want to speed up this process, pour it into a large bowl so the heat from the hot pan doesn't delay things. Juice your lemons well – you want all of the juice available!

Once cool, pour the herb syrup, lemon juice and apple juice through a sieve/strainer and into a mixing jug/pitcher (catching and discarding the boiled herbs). Mix well, then transfer the sorbet mixture to a freezerproof, sealable container. Remember that liquid expands a bit as it freezes so make sure your container is big enough.

Lots of recipes say you need to remove from the freezer and blitz multiple times whilst a sorbet freezes, but I don't bother with this. Let it fully freeze overnight, then follow my lead. Remove the frozen block of sorbet from the freezer, slice it up like you would brownies or flapjacks, then scoop out and put straight into a food processor (I find the high-powered ones don't work that well here, so a proper food processor is best if you have one) and give it a good old blitz for a couple of minutes until the sorbet is smooth. You may need to help the big chunks out a bit with a spoon; if so, do!

Transfer the sorbet back to the container and re-freeze for an hour. Then consume or store until you're ready. If you ever return and it's become a block of ice, just blitz again in a food processor and it'll be ready to go.

GOES WELL WITH Fresh, seasonal fruit or just on its own.

LEFTOVERS Will happily live in the freezer for a good while. If it looks a bit crystallized when you re-visit it, just blitz it up in a food processor to smooth out the sorbet.

TROPICAL FRUIT GRANITA

The world's quickest dessert, that's refreshing, flavoursome and literally two ingredients. You could even get away with just the cans of fruit if you didn't have any citrus fruit. I often whip a batch up and just leave it in the freezer for a refreshing, sweet snack in the sun, or serve it as a no-prep, icy dessert at a barbecue. It's the perfect choice when everyone is too full for a 'real' pudding, but you want a taste of something fruity to finish off the feast.

2 x 400-g/14-oz. cans of fruit, in juice or syrup (I think syrup is best for this)	Pineapple, peach, mango, apricot or pears are best
freshly squeezed juice of 1 lime	Lemon, orange or grapefruit, any citrus! If large, use half
SERVES 6–8	**TOTAL TIME 5 MINUTES, PLUS FREEZING AND SCRAPING**

Transfer one can of fruit (with its syrup or juice) to a high-powered food processor, then drain the second can and add only the fruit to the processor too (discarding the juice). Squeeze in the lime juice, then blitz until very smooth.

Transfer the mix to a freezerproof, sealable container and place in the freezer. After 1 hour use a fork to scrape the mix (this is to prevent it freezing into a solid block), seal and get it back in the freezer. Repeat this process for 5 hours (scraping every hour), then you'll have a great granita, ready to fork away at again and spoon into bowls.

GOES WELL WITH I like it served on top of yogurt and/or fresh fruit or you could spoon on top of an ice-filled cocktail!

LEFTOVERS Just keep it in the freezer and save for another day.

AUTUMN

BUTTERNUT SQUASH & CHICORY PASTA BAKE

I love a traditional lasagne and the nostalgic, knowing hug that it gives, and this pasta bake is a lovely, wholesome veggie alternative that equally hits the spot. You could try it with plenty of roasted veg, but I think sweet root veg work best.

800–900 g/1¾–2 lb. butternut squash, unpeeled	Carrots, sweet potato, celeriac/celery root, beetroot/beets, or a mix
50 g/3½ tablespoons butter	Essential
50 g/6 tablespoons plain/all-purpose flour	Wholemeal/whole-wheat or self-raising/rising
650 ml/2¾ cups whole milk	Any type of milk
40 g/½ cup grated Parmesan, plus extra to top	Any hard Italian cheese, such as Pecorino
2 heads chicory	Any bitter, winter leaf, such as endive
8–10 dried lasagne sheets	Fresh pasta sheets, about 160 g/5½ oz. in total
250 g/1¼ cups ricotta cheese	Any soft cheese, such as goat's cheese
20 g/1 oz. fresh basil	Fresh parsley or chives
sea salt and freshly ground pepper	
SERVES 6	*TOTAL TIME 1 HOUR 25 MINUTES*

Preheat the oven to 200°C fan/220°C/425°F/Gas 7.

Trim, then chop the butternut squash into 2–3-cm/¾–1¼-inch chunks (no need to peel). Add to a large baking sheet, season well, drizzle with a glug of olive oil and toss to coat. Place on the top shelf of the oven and roast for 35 minutes until tender and lightly caramelized.

Melt the butter in a medium saucepan set over a medium heat and once sizzling, add the flour. Mix very well and cook for a couple minutes. Next, add a splash of milk which will turn the roux firmer. Allow the milk to be absorbed before you add another generous splash. Continue this process until all the milk is used. Let the sauce cook and thicken for about 5 minutes, stirring constantly – it should end up with a custard-like thickness. Remove from the heat, add the Parmesan, stir to combine, then season very well (make sure you taste it).

Separate the chicory leaves, then cut them in half lengthways. Scatter a layer of squash on the base of a baking dish, followed by chicory, some dollops of ricotta randomly placed, then a layer of lasagne sheets. Top with the white sauce and a scattering of basil leaves (and their stalks, torn). Repeat the layers (starting with the roasted squash), continuing until you've used up all of the ingredients. Finish with a very generous scattering of basil leaves on the final layer of béchamel and an extra sprinkle of seasoning and Parmesan, too. Place on the middle shelf of the oven and bake for 40 minutes, until tender, golden brown on top and bubbling happily.

GOES WELL WITH Buttery peas or a lovely, fresh, crunchy salad.

LEFTOVERS Portion up and freeze, or just re-heat – everyone loves leftover pasta bake!

AUBERGINE RAGÙ

Whilst aubergines/eggplants are summer veg, this recipe sits in the autumn chapter because when the weather starts to turn, lots of us crave these richer, slow-cooked dishes. This one is a veggie-style ragù, it has depth but still has a light edge from the ripe tomatoes which I love. It's great for pasta but also fab to use in a lasagne, as a sandwich filling or, even better, with eggs as a shakshuka, or just on toast. It freezes really well, so make a double batch and save some for stress-free suppers when the weather is even colder.

3 aubergines/eggplants	Essential
2 red onions	More carrots or celery
2 carrots	More red onions or celery
2 celery sticks/stalks	More red onions or carrots
4 garlic cloves	Purée is fine, or use 2 teaspoons garlic powder
750 g/1 lb. 10 oz. fresh mixed tomatoes	Use 2 x 400-g/14-oz. cans of good-quality chopped tomatoes
400 ml/1¾ cups water	If using canned tomatoes, only use 200 ml/¾ cup water
1 teaspoon ground coriander	Any of the three spices can be substituted – try paprika, cayenne pepper, curry powder (will make it curried aubergine ragù though, but yum!), caraway, harissa paste
1 tablespoon cumin seeds	See above
1 teaspoon fennel seeds	See above
1 tablespoon tomato purée/paste	Can easily be omitted
130 ml/½ cup red wine	White wine or ½ quantity of red wine vinegar
olive oil	
sea salt and freshly ground pepper	
SERVES 4	*TOTAL TIME 1½ HOURS*

Preheat the oven to 210°C fan/200°C/400°F/Gas 6.

Chop the aubergines/eggplants into 4–5-cm/1¾–2-inch pieces and place on a large baking sheet. Drizzle some olive oil over, season well, then toss to coat. Place on the middle/top shelf of the preheated oven and roast for 1 hour, until golden brown and tender (this can be done in advance, by the way).

Meanwhile, halve, peel and thinly slice the onions and chop the carrots (no need to peel) and celery into 1–2-cm/½–¾-inch pieces. Heat a glug of olive oil in a large saucepan or casserole dish/Dutch oven, and once hot, add the soffrito (the prepared onions, carrots and celery). Fry gently for 20 minutes, stirring often.

Peel and thinly slice the garlic, roughly chop the tomatoes and measure the water. Once the soffrito is supple and glistening, add the garlic and spices, letting them fry for a couple of minutes until fragrant. Next, add the tomato purée/paste and mix well to combine. Let this 'cook out' (cooking off that rawness) for a couple of minutes, then pour in the wine and let it bubble away for a couple of minutes until most of the liquid has been absorbed. Pile in the tomatoes and pour in the water.

Bring the ragù mix up to the boil, then immediately reduce the heat to a gentle simmer and leave to gently cook for 50 minutes, stirring occasionally.

When the aubergines have had their time in the oven, add them to the sauce. Don't worry at what point this happens – just get them into the sauce as soon as they're roasted. Taste to check for seasoning, then serve.

GOES WELL WITH So many options here, but I like it served with pasta as a ragù, with rice, or just on toast with a fried egg on top.

LEFTOVERS This recipe freezes really well, but if you've only got a small portion left, try it stuffed in my Wonky Stuffed Flatbreads (page 42) or with Baked Eggs (page 17).

DRIED MUSHROOM RISOTTO

This is a super simple, pared-back risotto that allows the dried mushrooms to pump some umami and depth into the dish. As always with a risotto, make sure you season well – the starch needs it. The best part of making a risotto is adding the cold butter and Parmesan at the end, so take a minute to enjoy watching what happens in the pan as you do. A moment of meditative joy!

1.5 litres/6¼ cups chicken stock	Vegetable stock, or any meat stock
20 g/¾ oz. dried mushrooms	Fresh mushrooms – see method
1 large onion	Fennel or celery
3 garlic cloves	Purée or powder
350 g/1¾ cups risotto rice	I use Arborio or Carnaroli
50 ml/3½ tablespoons white wine	White wine vinegar, or cider would be nice here too
1 lemon	You do ideally want the lemon, but it can be omitted
20 g/1½ tablespoons salted butter, fridge cold	You need this to make it special, but it can be omitted or use unsalted
50 g/¾ cup grated Parmesan, plus extra to serve	You need this to make it special, but any hard cheese will do
unsalted butter, for cooking	Can use salted
sea salt and freshly ground pepper	
SERVES 4	**TOTAL TIME 45 MINUTES**

Add the stock (or water and stock jellies) and dried mushrooms (see note below if using fresh mushrooms) to a saucepan and bring to the boil. Once boiling, reduce the heat to very low and keep on the heat, not simmering, just hot. Pop a ladle in the pan so you're ready to go.

Halve, peel and finely chop the onion. Add a knob/pat of butter to a wide-bottomed saucepan and once hot, add the onion and fry gently for 10 minutes, until becoming soft.

Note: If you are using fresh mushrooms, thinly slice them and once the onions are tender, add them to the pan of onions. Let them release their moisture and take on a little colour, then continue with the method below.

Meanwhile, peel and grate the garlic. Once the onions have had their time, add the garlic and fry for 2 minutes, stirring often to avoid burning, then add the risotto rice. Mix well for a minute or so to coat the grains in the butter, then add the wine and let bubble away until most of the liquid has been absorbed.

Add the first ladle of chicken and mushroom stock, and let the risotto gently bubble, stirring often. Once the liquid has been almost completely absorbed, add another ladle of stock.

Settle the temperature to a gentle simmer, and once that ladleful has been almost completely absorbed again, add a third. Continue with this process until the risotto rice is almost al dente – this should take about 20 minutes.

When the rice is almost ready, season, taste and season again (remembering you're about to add Parmesan though, so don't go too mad on the salt).

Remove the pan from the heat, then add a final, scant ladleful of stock (scooping up any now-soft mushroom pieces still in the pan of stock). Grate the lemon zest into the risotto, then halve the lemon and add a squeeze of juice to the pan too. Also add the cold butter and Parmesan. Stir well, enjoy watching the butter and cheese melt and turn the risotto into velvety heaven. Taste to check for seasoning one final time, then pile onto plates immediately. Cut the remaining lemon half into wedges and take to the table, along with the Parmesan.

GOES WELL WITH Top with some salsa verde, add a few pieces of Confit Garlic (page 59) as garnish, or serve with a really fresh herb salad (any and all soft fresh herbs, tossed with a little olive oil and lemon juice).

LEFTOVERS Risotto Frittata (page 21) – make it the next day!

MINESTRONE WITH PECORINO & PARSLEY

Minestrone is my favourite soup – it's chunky, uses up what's in the fridge, there is pasta and a showering of cheese involved. It's also wonderful as leftovers, loaded up with more stock and any extras you want to throw in. You can add pancetta or bacon at the start if you wish.

1 large brown onion	Any onion, or use fennel, or top up on the other veg
2 garlic cloves	Purée or powder is fine, or omit
2 carrots	More onion, celery and leek
2 celery sticks/stalks	More onion, carrot and leek
1 leek	More onion, carrot and celery
200 g/7 oz. potato	Can be omitted
2 vine tomatoes	Any fresh tomato, or add 1 teaspoon tomato purée/paste with the garlic
400-g/14-oz. can of cannellini beans	Any cooked beans
80 g/3 oz. cavolo nero	Any leafy green, such as spinach, cabbage, kale
1 litre/4 cups chicken stock	Any stock, but chicken is best in my opinion
150 g/5½ oz. dried pasta	Any shape of dried pasta; fresh pasta is also fine, but add only 2 minutes before end of cooking
10 g/⅓ oz. parsley	Any fresh herb, or lemon zest and a squeeze of juice
40 g/1½ oz. Pecorino	Any hard cheese, or a dollop of mascarpone
butter, for frying	
extra virgin olive oil, for drizzling	
sea salt and freshly ground pepper	
SERVES 4–6	*TOTAL TIME 1 HOUR*

Halve, peel and thinly slice the onion. Heat a generous knob/pat of butter in a large casserole dish/Dutch oven on the hob/stovetop over a medium heat. Once the butter is gently sizzling, add the onion and fry gently for 10 minutes, until softening.

Peel and grate the garlic. Trim and finely slice the carrots, celery and leek. Chop the potato and tomatoes into 2-cm/¾-inch chunks. Drain and rinse the beans and finely shred the cavolo nero.

When the onions have had their time, add the garlic, carrot, celery, leek and potato. Mix to coat in the butter, then let them fry together for another 10 minutes, stirring often. Next, add the tomatoes, stock, beans and pasta. Bring to the boil and simmer for 8–10 minutes, until all the veg is tender, the pasta is al dente and it's smelling lovely.

When the soup only has 5 minutes left, add the cavolo nero and stir through, so it lightly cooks. Taste the soup – it'll probably need generous seasoning. Roughly chop the parsley and shave the Pecorino into crumbly shards. Transfer the soup to bowls and top with the cheese and parsley, finishing with a drizzle of extra virgin olive oil.

GOES WELL WITH Garlic-rubbed toast is my favourite.

LEFTOVERS Tear up the leftover garlicky bread suggested above, add it to the leftover minestrone and turn the soup into a ribollita.

ROAST CHICKEN & CIDER STEW

I love roast chicken and I love stews/casseroles/saucy meals, hence my love for this recipe. This is a one-dish fix, preferably made on a cold weekend. It's a super versatile recipe as the one ingredient you really do need is the chicken whilst the rest are completely changeable. I like making it with the herbs and veg listed below but they can be swapped out with so many alternatives. You could also make it just with celery and onion if you happen to have lots that need using up. The cider adds a lovely sweetness to the stock sauce and the leftovers are great blitzed up into a soup as well. Freeze the chicken carcass and any trimmings to make stock another time.

1 fennel bulb	All the vegetables in this dish can be swapped for pretty much anything
3 carrots	As above
2 onions	As above
2 garlic bulbs	Not necessary but they are gorgeous, so if you have them, add them whole
1 large whole chicken, 1.5–1.8 kg/3¼–4 lb.	Essential, but feel free to try this recipe with other birds
10 g/⅓ oz. (total weight) fresh thyme, oregano and sage	Any hardy herb is lovely with chicken
10 g/⅓ oz. parsley	Not essential. Chives or coriander/cilantro are nice here too
1 lemon, cut into wedges	Orange is nice, or just omit
40 g/3 tablespoons butter	Ideal, but you can omit if you wish or use oil
500-ml/18-oz can (hard) cider	If you have a smaller can of cider, make up the volume with extra chicken stock. Or use ½ apple juice/½ fizzy water for an alcohol-free recipe
500 ml/2 cups chicken stock	Chicken stock is best, but veg is fine too
400-g/14-oz. can of borlotti/ cranberry beans, drained and rinsed	Any cooked bean or legume
a splash of double/heavy cream (optional)	Single/light cream, sour cream, crème fraîche or mascarpone
olive oil, for roasting	
sea salt and freshly ground pepper	
SERVES 4	*TOTAL TIME 90 MINUTES*

Preheat the oven to 200°C fan/220°C/425°F/Gas 7.

Roughly chop the fennel, carrots and onions into 6–8-cm/2½–3¼-inch chunks or wedges, then scatter in the base of a large baking dish. Rip a few of cloves off one of the garlic bulbs and reserve; add the remaining garlic to the baking dish (no need to separate the cloves). Drizzle with some olive oil, sprinkle over a generous pinch of salt and pepper, then toss to coat.

Season the chicken (inside and out). Stuff all of the fresh herbs into the cavity, along with a couple of lemon wedges. Add the remaining wedges to the baking dish with the veg.

Thinly slice the reserved garlic cloves. Next, using your fingers, gently push inbetween the flesh and the skin (starting at the base of the breasts, leg end) to make space for some butter. Add chunks of butter and garlic slices in there and spread across the breast and over to the thigh flesh, if you can, trying not to rip the skin in the process. Place the chicken in the baking dish on top of the prepared veg and drizzle a little olive oil over the bird so it has some fat on the outside to help too.

When I roast chicken I use the three-turn process – this means you need to place the chicken on its side, laying on one leg for the first 20 minutes, then turn it so it lays on its other side for the next 20 minutes, and then finally onto its back (breasts up) for the last 20 minutes. So, get the bird onto one side, nestled amongst the veg. Roast on the top shelf in the preheated oven for 20 minutes, then remove from the oven, baste, turn the bird to the other side and back on the top shelf for another 20 minutes.

Remove from the oven, turn the bird onto its back, baste, then add the cider, stock and beans. Jiggle the veg, beans and liquid around a little to mix them up. Return the dish to the oven for another 20–30 minutes and finish roasting.

Once the time is up, check that the chicken is fully cooked (the juices should run clear from the cavity, or cut between the breast and leg and check the meat is not still pink) and if so, remove from the oven. If not, pop back in the oven until fully cooked.

Transfer the chicken to a resting board (cover loosely with foil if you want but I like crispy skin so I don't!) and return the cidery veg stew to the oven to cook for another 20 minutes, while the meat rests.

Carve the chicken and place the joints back on top of the stew and take the hot dish to the table. Spoon the hot stew over the chicken to warm it up a little and make sure everyone gets a ladle of the sauce along with the meat and veg. If you wish, a small slosh of cream poured in is divine, just saying...

GOES WELL WITH Mashed or baked potatoes and a crunchy winter salad.

LEFTOVERS So many possibilities! Sandwich, frittata or pasta options obviously, but also blitz any leftovers into a soup or fold them into a wintery chicken and roasted veg salad (warm up some of the cidery sauce and add it to your salad dressing, it's amazing).

CURRIED CHICKEN SCHNITZEL BAKE

This is a great one-dish bake with plenty of flavour but minimal fuss. It's really nice as a stand-alone meal with some greens on the side, or you could treat it like a baked curry and serve with rice, popadoms and a cucumber salad. I've prepared this recipe for two, but just double everything to serve four. It's important to avoid piling the chicken in the dish, so make sure all the pieces can lay snug but flat, in a single layer with each touching the base.

3 vine tomatoes	Any fresh tomatoes, halve large ones
100 g/½ cup natural yogurt	Any plain yogurt, or try coconut yogurt
1 tablespoon curry powder	Mild or hot, your choice; madras is great too
1 teaspoon ground turmeric	Can be omitted
¼ teaspoon dried chilli/hot red pepper flakes	Fresh thinly sliced chilli/chile, or chilli powder
1 teaspoon ground coriander	Crushed coriander or fennel seeds
1 teaspoon cumin seeds	½ teaspoon ground cumin or caraway
4 pieces of chicken, thighs and drumsticks (about 650 g/1 lb. 7 oz.)	Essential
65 g/1 cup breadcrumbs	Essential, but panko is fine
15 g/⅓ cup coconut flakes/chips	Lovely, but not essential
1 teaspoon garam masala	Any curry powder
sea salt and freshly ground pepper	
SERVES 2	**TOTAL TIME 1 HOUR**

Preheat the oven to 200°C fan/220°C/425°F/Gas 7.

Roughly chop the tomatoes and add them to a large mixing bowl. Now add the yogurt, curry powder, turmeric, chilli/hot red pepper flakes, coriander, cumin and a generous sprinkling of seasoning to the bowl and mix together. Next, add the chicken and coat in the curried tomato yogurt. Transfer the chicken and all of its marinade to a baking dish, so the chicken pieces are snug, but not on top of one another. Bake in the preheated oven for 50 minutes.

Meanwhile, make the topping. Add the breadcrumbs, coconut flakes/chips, garam masala and a good pinch of seasoning to a bowl and mix well to combine.

When the chicken has had its time, sprinkle the crumb mixture on top and return to the oven for a final 10 minutes. Remove from the oven and let it sit for 5 minutes, then serve.

GOES WELL WITH As I suggest above, just some greens (I like minty peas), or serve with some rice, popadoms and sliced cucumber.

LEFTOVERS Reheats well, just pop some foil on top to avoid the crumbed topping getting burnt second time round. Or slice up the chicken, reheat in a pan with extra chilli/chile and serve with potato wedges on the side for a crispy, crunchy curried chicken and chips!

BAVETTE STEAK WITH ROMESCO

I love making soups go further than just soup, and this sauce is as example of just that. Portion up any leftovers of Chipotle Red Pepper Soup (page 107), pop them in the freezer and grab a pot of them when needed for this easy, delicious romesco-style sauce. For the steak, I've chosen the bavette cut, but have this sauce with whatever you like – it's great with any steak, most meats and plenty of veg or fish, too. It's also really nice with ham on toast, as I discovered whilst writing this book!

2 bavette steaks	Any steak you like; lamb or pork, too
3 tablespoons olive oil	Rapeseed/canola oil, or a mix of extra virgin and olive or vegetable oil
½ teaspoon cracked black pepper	White pepper or crushed mixed peppercorns
4 garlic cloves, bashed	Some fresh rosemary for marinating instead
100 g/1¼ cups flaked/slivered almonds	Essential
1 teaspoon smoked paprika	Sweet paprika is fine, or try a small pinch of mild chilli/chili powder
1 tablespoon sherry vinegar	Red wine vinegar, cider or white wine vinegar (in that order)
200 ml/¾ cup Chipotle Red Pepper Soup (page 107)	You do ideally need the leftover soup, but could use jarred roasted peppers
60 ml/4 tablespoons extra virgin olive oil	Normal olive oil will do
a knob/pat of butter (optional)	
sea salt	
SERVES 2	***TOTAL TIME 20 MINUTES, PLUS MARINATING***

Marinate the bavette steaks in the olive oil, black pepper and garlic cloves for 30 minutes, at room temperature.

Whilst the meat sits, make the romesco sauce. Place half the almonds in a frying pan/skillet over a medium heat. Toast for a couple minutes, tossing occasionally until golden. Transfer to a food processor, then repeat with the remaining almonds. Once all the toasted almonds are in the food processor, add the paprika and blitz until roughly chopped and a similar texture to breadcrumbs.

Next, add the sherry vinegar, cold soup and a good pinch of seasoning to the food processor and blitz once more. Let the mixture combine, then slowly pour in the extra virgin olive oil while it continues to blend. Taste to check for seasoning and if necessary, season and blitz again, then taste a final time. You want there to be some texture in there, so don't worry about it looking a little lumpy – it's meant to be like that. Transfer to a small serving dish and set aside.

Bring a large frying pan/skillet (or a griddle pan, or use a barbecue) to a very high heat, in fact it should be smoking. Once hot, quickly season the steaks all over with sea salt, then add to the pan and flash fry for 90 seconds on each side. Don't move them around in the pan and don't remove the pan from the heat source. Once you have turned the steaks, let them have another 90 seconds. If you prefer your steaks more well done, fry for 2–3 minutes on each side. If you like, add a knob/pat of butter to the pan and spoon the fizzing butter over the steak, but to be honest, these steaks benefit from such a short cooking time that I often don't bother with the butter when frying bavette.

Transfer the steaks from the pan on to a plate, loosely covering to keep warm, and let rest for 5 minutes. Serve the steaks with the romesco sauce and devour.

GOES WELL WITH Lemon and Pecorino Polenta Fries (page 151) and a simple salad of watercress or lamb's lettuce.

LEFTOVERS Slice the steak and add to the Tofu Noodles with Mushrooms and Marmite (page 77). Use any leftover romesco sauce in sandwiches, as a dip or spread onto crackers with some Marinated Feta (page 29) or Labneh (page 33). You could even try it with the Breaded Corn on the Cob (page 119) and use it instead of the miso mayo mix.

SAUSAGES WITH APPLE, ONION, PEARL BARLEY & A MARMALADE DRESSING

Pearl barley is probably my favourite grain. It's robust, with a good bite and has a lovely nutty flavour. Grains in general are welcoming vessels to so many accompaniments. I have enjoyed many versions of this recipe over the years, but here is a particularly favourite one, perfect for autumn. Hopefully you have the ingredients to enjoy my original recipe, but if not, no worries! The main aim is to combine grains, apples, sausages, herbs and a sweet dressing. Use whatever apples you've got (it's lovely whether they go really mushy or remain a firmer roasted wedge) and you can even try it with pears, too.

2 apples	Any sort of apple you have, or pears
2 red onions	Any onion, shallot, spring onion/scallion or leek slices
1 garlic bulb	Add 1 teaspoon purée to dressing if that's the only garlic you have
12 sausages	Essential
8 sprigs of sage	Oregano, rosemary or thyme stalks
200 g/1 heaped cup pearl barley	Any grain, but bulgur wheat or buckwheat are lovely instead
10 g/⅓ oz. parsley	Fresh basil or chives
MARMALADE DRESSING	
2 tablespoons marmalade	Any sweet chutney works – mango chutney is good
60 ml/4 tablespoons extra virgin olive oil	Normal olive oil, rapeseed/canola or walnut oil work well too
1 tablespoon grainy mustard	Dijon mustard is fine, or just omit
60 ml/4 tablespoons cider vinegar	Any vinegar will do here
olive oil, for roasting	
sea salt and freshly ground pepper	
SERVES 4	**TOTAL TIME 50 MINUTES**

Preheat the oven to 200°C fan/220°C/425°F/Gas 7.

Quarter the apples, remove the core and cut each quarter into 3 wedges. Quarter the onions, peel and cut each of these quarters in half, to make thinner wedges. Break up the garlic bulb into cloves, but leave the skins on.

Place the sausages (giving them a quick stab with a knife), apple and onion wedges on a large baking sheet lined with parchment paper, along with the sage stalks, garlic cloves and a good drizzle of olive oil and seasoning. Toss the ingredients to coat and mingle, then place on the top shelf of the preheated oven. Bake for 40 minutes until all the ingredients are cooked through, tender and caramelized (turn all the ingredients half way through cooking).

Meanwhile, cook the pearl barley according to the packet instructions, then drain and rinse under cold water. Place in a large salad bowl with a small drizzle of olive oil and a generous pinch of seasoning. Toss to combine and set aside. Roughly chop or tear the parsley and add to the pearl barley bowl.

Make the dressing by adding the dressing ingredients, along with a good pinch of seasoning, to your smallest saucepan and bring to the boil. Once bubbling, remove from the heat and taste to check for seasoning. It should look really oily. When you're happy with the flavour, just leave it on the side and you can reheat it just before serving. If there are any big chunks of orange rind, they can easily be broken up with a spoon once hot. Note that the dressing on its own can taste quite tart and intense, but once it is folded through all the sweet roasted items and nutty grains, it evens out and works really well. If you're unsure, just add it gradually to the dish and see what you think.

Once the baking sheet items are ready, slice the sausages in half at an angle, then pile those, along with all of the other roasted ingredients, into the salad bowl and toss to combine. The sage stalks may need fishing out, but don't worry too much. Give the dressing a quick 30 seconds over some heat, then pour over, toss once more and serve the warm sausage and barley dish immediately.

GOES WELL WITH This is a fairly well rounded, stand-alone dish so it really doesn't need anything more. Having said that, I do really like Tartare Sauce (page 64) with this dish and an extra handful of salad. Other than that, you're good to go!

LEFTOVERS Heats up very nicely in the oven as it is. I wouldn't really mess around with this one, it doesn't need it.

GOES WELL WITH Bavette Steak with Romesco (page 145), Tartare Sauce (page 64) or Chicken, Mango and Cucumber Ciabatta (page 115).

LEFTOVERS Really lovely just reheated in the oven until piping hot and crisp, then either enjoyed as fries again or broken up into croutons and scattered over a salad or dip, or folded through roasted veg and grains.

LEMON & PECORINO POLENTA FRIES

These fries are just so good. They're the perfect do-ahead side and they go so crispy, making them the ultimate 'chip' for a crispy, crunchy addict like me. There's lots of savouriness in the Pecorino and veg stock, so be sparing with the salt (I just add a sprinkle before baking – you can always add but you can't take away!). Try loading the polenta/ cornmeal with lots of different flavours – it's great with herbs, spices, cheeses and the like.

400 ml/1¾ cups vegetable stock	Chicken stock is fine
100 ml/⅓ cup whole milk	Any milk or just use 500 ml/2 cups stock
50 g/2 oz. Pecorino	Parmesan, Grana Padano or any hard cheese
1 lemon	Try some sumac, or a little lime juice (but omit the zest)
150 g/1 cup polenta/cornmeal, plus extra for coating	Essential
olive oil, for baking	
sea salt and freshly ground pepper	
SERVES 4	*TOTAL TIME 45 MINUTES, PLUS COOLING*

Line a large baking sheet with parchment paper. Add the vegetable stock and milk (with a good grind of pepper) to a medium saucepan and bring to just below the boil.

While the liquid heats up, finely grate the cheese. Zest the lemon and then cut into wedges.

When the liquid has come to temperature, add the polenta/cornmeal and stir continuously, until all the liquid has been absorbed. Continue stirring constantly until the mix is thick and coming away from the side of the pan. It should only take a minute or two.

Remove from the heat and immediately add the Pecorino and lemon zest to the polenta. Stir very well to combine, then pile onto the lined baking sheet and spread out so it's smooth and about 1 cm/½ inch thick. This bit is really satisfying, enjoy! Leave the polenta to cool for about 15 minutes.

Preheat the oven to 220°C fan/240°C/450°F/Gas 8.

Once cool, lift the block of polenta up using the parchment paper and place on a chopping board. Slice the block up into fries – I like cutting 1-cm/½-inch thick, long fries as this makes for super crispy 'French fries'.

Using the same baking sheet (now without the parchment paper) sprinkle a little dry polenta over the sheet, then spread out the fries on top. Sprinkle a little more dry polenta on top, and finish with a squeeze of lemon juice, a scant sprinkle of sea salt and a drizzle of olive oil. Place on the top shelf of the preheated oven and bake for 30 minutes, until very crispy. Serve with the spare lemon wedges alongside for squeezing and a little extra grated Pecorino on top.

GINGER RICE

I love rice and I love ginger. This is a kind of egg-fried rice dish, but with loads of ginger. I don't tend to peel ginger these days, and for good reason. While it's not that pretty in a pan, the skin brings a gentle extra bit of heat and I love it. Less waste, more flavour.

1 shallot	Any onion, or omit
40-g/1½-oz. piece of fresh ginger	Essential
250 g/9 oz. cooked rice	Any type of cooked rice
1 egg	Egg is great, but can be omitted. Or crumble in some tofu
1 teaspoon sesame oil	Not essential, can omit
rapeseed/canola oil, for frying	
sea salt and freshly ground pepper	
SERVES 2	*TOTAL TIME 15 MINUTES*

Halve, peel and thinly slice the shallot, then trim and thinly slice the ginger into matchsticks (no need to peel).

Add a good drizzle of rapeseed/canola oil to a medium-sized, non-stick frying pan/skillet set over a medium-high heat and once hot, add the shallot and ginger. Fry for 5 minutes, until becoming slightly golden and crisp.

Next, add the rice to the pan and cook, stirring very often, for 5 minutes, until piping hot. It's really important to bring the rice right up to temperature, so don't shortcut this part. Give the pan items a sprinkling of seasoning at this point, too.

Next, push the rice to the side, crack the egg into the pan and loosely scramble it. Once it's almost cooked, bring the rice back into the centre of the pan and combine all the ingredients. Add the sesame oil, then season once more, taste and season again if needed, then remove from the heat and serve.

GOES WELL WITH I really like this with some steak or poached chicken, or just with some frozen peas and spinach stirred through it, fresh coriander/cilantro and a jiggle of soy sauce and chilli/chili oil.

LEFTOVERS Reheats well, but only once and make sure, as before, the rice is piping hot.

SALTED BUTTER & CINNAMON BISCUITS

These are really great, they're like a mini cheesecake but in biscuit form, with the most amazing filling. You can make both parts ahead of time, so no need feel like you have to prepare them in unison. There will be a bit of leftover salted butter sauce too (the sauce on its own, not mixed in with the cream cheese), but you can store it in a sealed container in the fridge for a couple of weeks, or freeze for a month or so.

SALTED BUTTER CHEESECAKE FILLING	
25 g/1¾ tablespoons unsalted butter	Salted butter is fine, but just halve the quantity of sea salt
25 g/2 tablespoons dark brown soft sugar	Any sugar is absolutely fine, but I like brown sugar best
75 ml/⅓ cup double/heavy cream	Can use single/light cream
¼ teaspoon sea salt	Can use ⅛ teaspoon table salt
100 g/½ cup minus 1 tablespoon cream cheese	Can use mascarpone
SHORTBREAD BISCUITS	
130 g/9 tablespoons salted butter, softened	Unsalted butter is fine. Add a pinch of sea salt!
50 g/heaping ⅓ cup icing/confectioner's sugar	Caster/superfine or golden caster sugar will work
½ teaspoon ground cinnamon	Mixed spice or ground allspice
160 g/1½ cups plain/all-purpose flour	Essential
MAKES 12	*TOTAL TIME 45 MINUTES, PLUS CHILLING AND COOLING*

Make the salted butter sauce first as it needs a while to cool. Add the butter, sugar, cream and sea salt to a saucepan set over a low-medium heat and whisk continuously for about 3 minutes as the ingredients gently melt and meld into one another. Once all the sugar has dissolved and the ingredients have combined, bring the mixture up to the boil and let bubble very vigorously for 2 minutes. Remove from the heat and let the bubbles subside. Set aside and let the salted butter sauce cool.

To make the shortbread biscuits add the butter, sugar and cinnamon to a large mixing bowl, then briefly combine using an electric, hand-held whisk until well combined. Then add the flour until just combined and looking like chunky, fudgy breadcrumbs.

Tip the mix onto a clean work surface and bring together with your hands into a rough log about 6 cm/2½ inches in diameter. You can handle it a little, but don't 'knead'; the soft butter will help bring everything together easily and if you play with the dough too much, you'll end up with tough shortbread. Transfer the log onto a large piece of parchment paper (or clingfilm/

GOES WELL WITH A hot drink, a sofa and a roaring fire.

LEFTOVERS If the biscuits are already 'built', store them in the fridge and consume asap. They'll last for several days but the biscuits will go soft. The better alternative is to store the biscuits and filling separately.

plastic wrap) and roll into a tight log, tying up both ends to seal. Transfer the log to the freezer and let firm up for 20 minutes.

Preheat the oven to 180°C fan/200°C/400°F/Gas 6.

Line your largest baking sheet with parchment paper, then collect your shortbread biscuit log from the freezer. Unwrap the log, and slice it into discs 5 mm/¼ inch thick – you should get about 24. Lay them out on the baking sheet, transfer straight to the top shelf of the preheated oven and bake for 12–15 minutes, until cooked, sandy and slightly coloured at the edges. Place the baking sheet on a cooling rack and leave to cool.

Once the salted butter sauce has come down to room temperature, place the cream cheese in a mixing bowl and add 90 g/3 oz. sauce, mixing well to combine. Spread the filling onto the base of half the biscuits, then top them with another biscuit – like a Jammy Dodger or an Oreo! There you have it, they're ready.

Note: If you're not serving them immediately, store the biscuits and filling separately and put them together just before serving. These biscuits are best stored in a sealed container at room temperature, and the filling is best stored in a sealed container in the fridge.

This recipe makes more sauce than you need, but freeze what you don't use (in a plastic, sealable container) and it is really great de-frosted and warmed up as a salted butter sauce for ice cream. Or make more biscuits!

LEMONGRASS POACHED PEARS

Autumn brings with it my favourite fruits – pears, apples and citrus fruits. This recipe calls for a few pears, some sugar and spices – I've used Thai and Indian fragrant spices to freshen up the sweetness of the poached pears and their syrup. The recipe below, like this entire book, is a guide – use what you've got and see what you like best. It's best for the pears to be pretty ripe, but still fairly firm to the touch. A too-ripe pear will most likely break down during cooking, so go for a firmer fruit if you have a choice.

1 lemongrass stalk, bashed	Dried lemongrass or more ginger
zest of 1 lemon	Orange or lime
200 g/1 cup caster/granulated sugar	Any type of sugar; golden caster sugar is first choice
4 cardamom pods, bashed	A couple of cloves, or a pinch of mixed spice
1 star anise	Experiment with a scattering of fennel or caraway seeds
30-g/1-oz. piece of fresh ginger, roughly sliced	Try a cinnamon stick or two
1 litre/4 cups water	
4 pears	Conference/Bosc are best but use what you've got
SERVES 4	**TOTAL TIME 45 MINUTES COOKING, 30 MINUTES COOLING**

Add all the ingredients, apart from the pears, to a large saucepan and bring to the boil. Stir, making sure all the sugar has dissolved.

Make a cartouche (a piece of parchment paper that sits directly on the surface of the liquid rather than using a normal pan lid) – cut a circle of paper the same size as the diameter of your pan, then scrunch it up and stretch it out again (scrunching it up makes it more pliable).

When the poaching liquor has almost come to the boil, core the pears by cutting around the base with a small, sharp knife and scooping out the core to a depth of roughly 2 cm/¾ inch, then peel.

Once boiling, add the pears to the pan (if they're not covered, add more water until they are), then reduce the temperature to a very low simmer, place the cartouche on top and leave to cook for 25 minutes, or until tender.

When cooked, remove from the heat and let the whole pan cool for about 30 minutes. Gently scoop out the pears and place in a serving dish with the cartouche on top, then put the pan of poaching liquor over a super high heat and bring to a rolling boil. Once vigorously bubbling, leave it on the heat for about 20 minutes until the liquor has reduced by half and become a loose syrup. Remove from the heat and serve, pouring the syrup over the pears.

You can also store the cooked pears in their syrup in the fridge for up to 3 days.

GOES WELL WITH They're great on their own or serve with vanilla ice cream.

LEFTOVERS Serve on porridge or yogurt for breakfast. They're lovely sliced up and served in a bowl with a cheese board, too.

WINTER

APPLE & CUMIN SLAW WITH LIME DRESSING

I love winter fruit in salads, so here is a fresh, crunchy winter slaw that's half fruit bowl/half fridge. It can be made in advance too, and if you don't have an apple, try it with something else – see below for suggested alternatives.

1 teaspoon cumin seeds	Caraway seeds (but only ½ teaspoon), or crushed and toasted coriander seeds
250 g/9 oz. white or savoy cabbage	Any sort of cabbage, spring greens, cavolo nero or kale
1 apple, cored (skin on)	Pear, orange segments, grapefruit segments, grapes
freshly grated zest and juice of 2 limes	Lemon is fine here
80 g/⅓ cup Greek yogurt	Natural/plain yogurt of any kind
1 garlic clove, grated	Garlic purée or ¼ teaspoon garlic powder
2 tablespoons cider vinegar	Any vinegar
1 tablespoon wholegrain mustard	Any mustard
10 g/⅓ oz. parsley, roughly chopped	Coriander/cilantro, chives, dill, or a combination
sea salt and freshly ground pepper	
SERVES 4 AS A SIDE	*TOTAL TIME 10 MINUTES*

Add the cumin seeds to a frying pan/skillet set over a low-medium heat and lightly toast in the pan for 2–3 minutes, tossing often, until fragrant and slightly darkened in colour. Remove from the heat and let cool.

Finely shred the cabbage and thinly slice the apple and transfer to a mixing bowl. Douse in the lime zest and juice, tossing to coat the apple, then pile in the remaining ingredients, along with a good pinch of salt and pepper. Mix very well for about 3–4 minutes with your hands – really get in there! Finally, taste to check for seasoning.

GOES WELL WITH Mustard Turkey and Mushroom Crumble (page 166) or Roasties Take Two (page 165). It's lovely with roasted ham, too.

LEFTOVERS This slaw will last a day or two in the fridge, but it will get softer and release more liquid, so it's best to keep it chilled and then continue to treat it as a side dish or sandwich filler/toast topper.

ROASTIES TAKE TWO

Roast potatoes are a household favourite in so many homes, and I make them in vast quantities. Leftover roasties, or any crispy, crunchy potato for that matter, are brilliant re-heated and re-crisped. So, get going with this winter salad and see what you think!

300 g/10½ oz. leftover roast potatoes	Any cooked, previously crunchy potato, or wedges or chips/fries
½ teaspoon cayenne pepper	Smoked paprika or small pinch of chilli/chili powder
80 g/3 oz. giant wholewheat couscous	Any grain – bulgur wheat or buckwheat work well
1 carrot	Segment an orange or tangerine
100 g/3½ oz. radicchio (medium head)	Endive, chicory or rocket/arugula
2 tangerines	Clementine, orange, pomelo or even grapefruit
3 tablespoons extra virgin olive oil	Ideally use extra virgin olive oil, but normal is fine
200 g/7 oz. burrata	Mozzarella is the best alternative, or mild, soft goat's cheese
olive oil, for roasting	
sea salt and freshly ground pepper	
SERVES 4	**TOTAL TIME 20 MINUTES**

Preheat the oven to 220°C fan/240°C/475°F/Gas 9.

Place the roast potatoes on a baking sheet and using a fork, squish each one to flatten it slightly and create some more edges for crisping up. Sprinkle with the cayenne pepper, drizzle with a little oil and season. Re-roast on the top shelf of the preheated oven for 15 minutes, until golden-brown and very crispy.

Meanwhile, boil the giant couscous according to the packet instructions, then drain well, rinse under cold water and set aside.

Peel the carrot into ribbons, separate the radicchio leaves and add them all to a large salad bowl. Once the couscous and potatoes are ready, add them to the bowl too. Finally, juice the tangerines over the salad, followed by the extra virgin olive oil and a good pinch of seasoning. Toss all the ingredients together, then loosely tear the burrata over the top. Serve immediately.

GOES WELL WITH I think this salad is the perfect accompaniment to a steak. Or have it with some of Hal's Tahini and Yogurt Dressing (page 58), if you want a punchier sauce.

LEFTOVERS This salad is best consumed when fresh, but if you have leftovers, maybe just replace any very soggy radicchio leaves and top up with some fresh leaves. It's lovely livened up and served as an open sandwich on some warm ciabatta or focaccia.

MUSTARD TURKEY & MUSHROOM CRUMBLE

Gather your leftover Christmas or Thanksgiving turkey and get making this savoury crumble. It's a welcome change from turkey sandwiches and we all need some inspiration for the day after, so try it out and see what you think. I like making this in individual pie pots.

FILLING	
1 onion	Any onion or use celery, fennel or carrot
150 g/5½ oz. baby button mushrooms	Any mushrooms, or use more turkey
5 g/¼ oz. fresh rosemary	Thyme or oregano are lovely, or parsley
3 garlic cloves	Purée or powder will do
150 g/5½ oz. Brussels sprouts	Any type of cabbage or peas
250–300 g/9–10½ oz. leftover cooked turkey	Chicken or pork; for vegetarians, use cooked root veg
1 tablespoon plain/all-purpose flour	Any flour
100 ml/7 tablespoons white wine	Cider, sherry or any vinegar
2 tablespoons Dijon mustard	Grainy mustard or 1 tablespoon mustard powder
250 ml/1 cup single/light cream	Double/heavy cream, mascarpone, sour cream or whole milk
200 ml/¾ cup water	
butter, for frying	
CRUMBLE	
25 g/1¾ tablespoons butter	Salted or unsalted is fine
50 g/6 tablespoons plain/all-purpose flour	Ideally use plain/all-purpose flour, but wholemeal/whole-wheat also works well
15 g/2 tablespoons rolled oats	Ideally use oats, but if not add more flour or ground almonds
10 g/⅓ oz. Parmesan	Any hard cheese, such as Pecorino, Cheddar, etc
sea salt and freshly ground pepper	
SERVES 4	*TOTAL TIME 1 HOUR 20 MINUTES*

4 individual pie dishes

Preheat the oven to 200°C fan/220°C/425°F/Gas 7.

Halve, peel and thinly slice the onion. Halve the mushrooms. Remove the rosemary leaves from their stalks and finely chop, discarding the stalks. Peel, then thinly slice the garlic cloves.

Add a generous knob/pat of butter to a large saucepan set over a medium heat and once hot, add the onion and mushrooms. Fry for 5 minutes, stirring often, until softening and starting to caramelize.

GOES WELL WITH Steamed greens, and I actually love this with oven chips/ fries on the side…

LEFTOVERS Just re-heat and scoff. No better way with this one.

Meanwhile, thinly slice the sprouts and tear the cooked turkey into bite-sized chunks.

When the onion and mushrooms have had 5 minutes, add the sliced sprouts, stir to combine and fry for another 5 minutes, until softening. Next, add the rosemary, garlic and a good pinch of seasoning to the pan and fry for a couple of minutes, until fragrant. Stir often to avoid the garlic burning.

Add the flour to the pan, stir to coat all the ingredients and let it 'cook out' for a minute, then add the wine and let it bubble away until it's almost fully absorbed. Add the mustard, cream, water and turkey. Stir very well to fully combine, while it comes to the boil. Taste to check for seasoning (it will need a generous amount), then remove from the heat and divide evenly between your pie dishes.

Next, make the crumble. Chop the butter into small cubes, then add to a large mixing bowl with the flour and a pinch of seasoning. Rub between your fingers to make rough, sandy breadcrumbs, then add in the oats and grate in the Parmesan. Mix it all together to combine, then scatter over the mustard turkey filling in the pie dishes.

Place the dishes on a large baking sheet, then transfer to the top shelf of the preheated oven and bake for 40 minutes until cooked, golden and bubbling away.

Let sit for a couple of minutes out of the oven, then serve.

CAULIFLOWER & LEEK GRATIN

Cauliflower cheese has got to be one of the most comforting side dishes ever. This is a fairly traditional version, but I've pre-roasted the veg to give it more depth of flavour and added a herby, garlicky, crunchy topping because, why not! Add extras into the mix if you like, more greens, cooked potatoes, some leftover pasta, cooked meats such as bacon, chorizo, chicken, whatever you like really. I often add leftover roast potatoes too and then you've got a good hefty gratin that sits perfectly alongside a roast chicken and some crunchy salad – simply lovely!

200 g/7 oz. cheese (I use 100 g/3½ oz. Cheddar, then a mix of others)	Cheddar, Emmental, mozzarella, blue, brie, Parmesan, etc
5 g/¼ oz. each fresh oregano and sage	Rosemary (finely chopped), parsley or thyme
1 cauliflower head	Essential
3 leeks	Fennel is lovely, potato or onion wedges too
50 g/3½ tablespoons salted butter	Essential
50 g/heaped ⅓ cup plain/all-purpose flour	Use any flour
700 ml/3 cups whole milk	Any milk will do
40 g/¾ cup breadcrumbs	You can leave these out, or use some broken crackers
10 cloves Confit Garlic (page 59)	Not essential, but really delicious if you have some
olive oil, for roasting	
sea salt and freshly ground pepper	
SERVES 4–6	*TOTAL TIME 1 HOUR*

Preheat the oven to 200°C fan/220°C/425°F/Gas 7.

Grate the cheese, separate the herb leaves from their stalks and set both aside.

Tear the leaves off the cauliflower (but don't throw them away), cut the head of the cauliflower into medium florets and chop the stalk into chunks. Trim, rinse, then slice the leeks into 6-cm/2½-inch chunks. Add them all (including the leaves and stalk) to your largest baking sheet and drizzle with a glug of olive oil and a good pinch of seasoning. Toss to coat, then place on the top shelf of the preheated oven to roast for 30 minutes.

Meanwhile, make your sauce. Add the butter to a medium saucepan set over a medium heat and let melt. Once gently sizzling, add the flour and mix vigorously to combine. Let this roux 'cook out' for about 3–4 minutes until it becomes a 'brown roux' (you want it a nice shade of butterscotch), then add a first splash of the milk and whisk. This will cause it to thicken.

Once that milk has all been absorbed and become stiff, add another glug of milk, and continue to do so, gradually, whisking continuously. Once all the milk is in the pan, it's time to just stand there and gently stir until the sauce thickens. It'll take about 5 minutes or so. When your sauce has a lovely, custard-like thickness, remove from the heat and fold through ¾ of the grated cheese. Taste to check for seasoning, you'll probably need to add more salt and pepper. Don't be shy, seasoning maketh a gratin! When you're happy with the flavour, set aside until the veg is roasted and out of the oven.

Meanwhile, mix the remaining grated cheese, herbs and breadcrumbs, with a pinch more seasoning. This is your topping.

Remove the baking sheet from the oven, transfer the roasted veg to a baking dish and then pour all of the cheese sauce on top. Sprinkle over the topping, then finish with the confit garlic cloves – just dot them on top randomly.

Bake the gratin on the top shelf of the preheated oven for 25 minutes until golden brown, bubbling and crisp.

GOES WELL WITH It's actually a great meal just with a very crunchy and fresh salad and some gammon on the side, or a roast lunch accompaniment. You know the deal with cauliflower cheese though... welcome in most scenarios.

LEFTOVERS It freezes well, so you could portion up into smaller roasting dishes, or just reheat and serve with different accompaniments. Alternatively, blitz it up into a cheesy soup topped with some crispy bacon lardons.

SOY & SPRING ONION GRILLED FISH

This is such a quick and simple recipe, ready in a flash. Purists will wince, but those microwave packs of rice are this recipe's best friend. I also think they're a brilliant product, so grab one of those pouches and prepare some quick rice while the fish grills/broils. I have tried this recipe with plenty of different varieties of fish, it works well with so many of them, but you do need a chunky fillet so it doesn't overcook. Skin or no skin, white and meaty, or luscious and oily – your choice!

250 g/9 oz. chunky fish fillets	Cod, hake, haddock, salmon, monkfish… any!
4 spring onions/scallions	Shallot or leeks, pak choi or cabbage, thinly sliced
½ teaspoon Chinese five spice	A pinch of fennel seeds, ground cloves and ginger
1 teaspoon black rice vinegar	Any vinegar
2 tablespoons sesame oil	Any oil
2 tablespoons soy sauce	Essential
1 teaspoon sesame seeds	Ideal, but can omit
1 teaspoon honey	Anything sweet – agave, date syrup or brown sugar
rice, to serve	
sesame oil, for greasing	
SERVES 2	*TOTAL TIME 20 MINUTES*

Preheat your grill/broiler to its highest setting.

Cut the fish into about 6-cm/2½-inch chunks. Trim and then halve the spring onions/scallions lengthways and then widthways. Place all of the ingredients in a mixing bowl and toss well to coat and combine.

Line a baking sheet with foil, then rub a little oil onto the foil, to prevent the fish from sticking. Next, tip the marinated fish and spring onions onto the foil, spreading them out so everything sits in a single layer and isn't crowded together.

Place on the top shelf of the preheated oven and grill/broil for 8 minutes, until the fish is cooked through, and the spring onions are soft, but slightly charred.

While the fish is cooking, prepare the rice according to the packet instructions. Serve the fish on a bed of rice.

GOES WELL WITH Rice and chilli/chili oil, I just love the simplicity! Or try it with my Ginger Rice (page 152).

LEFTOVERS The fish can be reheated to make a fishy stir-fry.

LEFTOVER MASSAMAN CURRY

I love making this the day after serving some sort of beef – roast beef, steaks, even mince/ ground beef or koftas (which sounds weird, but it works). The essentials are the flavourings and coconut milk, as the filling/chunky parts are very interchangeable (and you can add more veg if you want to bulk it out). There are a lot of ingredients, but it really is worth it.

CURRY PASTE	
1 shallot	Any onion is fine, but if large, only use half
1 lemongrass stalk	A bit of dried lemongrass is fine, or omit
3 garlic cloves	Essential, but can use purée
25-g/1-oz. piece of fresh ginger	Essential, but can use paste, purée or ground
3 cardamom pods (seeds only)	A pinch each of ground cinnamon and nutmeg
1 star anise	Ground star anise, or ¼ teaspoon Chinese five spice
1 teaspoon coriander seeds	Ground coriander or more cumin
1 teaspoon cumin seeds	Ground cumin or more coriander seeds
½ teaspoon chilli/hot red pepper flakes	Chilli/chili powder, cayenne pepper or some chopped fresh chilli/chile
¼ teaspoon ground cinnamon	A grating or pinch of ground nutmeg will do
3 dried makrut lime leaves	Just leave these out, or add some lime zest if you have some
40 g/⅓ cup roasted salted peanuts	Any sort of peanuts, but if they're not roasted, add salt
1 teaspoon galangal paste	I've made this curry without and it's really great still
1 teaspoon shrimp paste	Fine to omit this
CURRY	
1 onion	Any sort of onion, or some celery or leek
220 g/8 oz. leftover beef or steak	If using raw beef, cook for longer. Or use cooked chicken, pork or lamb
200 g/7 oz. leftover roast potatoes	Any cooked potato; butternut squash also works well
400-g/14-oz. can of coconut milk	Essential
2 tablespoons fish sauce	Soy sauce or tamari
1 teaspoon brown sugar	Any sort of sugar, but palm sugar is really the best
10 g/½ oz. coriander/cilantro	Thai basil, parsley or even mint
1 red chilli/chile (optional)	Optional, but more dried chilli/hot red pepper flakes or chilli/chili oil
1 lime	½ lemon, or omit
rapeseed/canola oil, for frying	
sea salt and freshly ground pepper	

SERVES 4 *TOTAL TIME 45 MINUTES*

GOES WELL WITH Jasmine rice and
a cold beer!

LEFTOVERS Heated up, but remember
the beef is already reheated so only
once and make sure the whole curry is
properly piping hot before consuming.

First make the curry paste. Halve, peel and finely chop the shallot. Bash then finely chop the lemongrass. Peel and thinly slice the garlic. Slice the ginger into matchsticks (no need to peel). Add all the spices, lime leaves and peanuts to a spice grinder (or use a pestle and mortar, grinding the spices first, then add the peanuts) and blitz (or pound) until broken down fully.

Heat a large, non-stick frying pan/skillet over a high heat and once hot (no oil added yet), add the ground spices, shallot, lemongrass, ginger, garlic, galangal paste and shrimp paste. Stirring very often, let it dry-fry for 5 minutes, until the chunky curry paste is very fragrant and slightly charred too.

Meanwhile, halve, peel and thinly slice the onion, slice the beef into bite-sized strips and halve any really big roast potatoes. Next, add the potato, onion and a glug of rapeseed/canola oil to the curry paste in the pan and fry for 5 minutes, stirring very often to avoid the curry paste burning – you might want to reduce the heat slightly at this point. Next, add the coconut milk, fish sauce and sugar to the pan and bring to the boil. Once boiling, reduce the heat to a gentle simmer and let lightly bubble for 10 minutes.

Roughly chop the coriander/cilantro and slice the chilli/chile. Taste the curry to check for seasoning, then add the beef to the pan and let simmer for a final 3–5 minutes. You just want to warm the beef up, not over-cook it, which would make it tough. Squeeze in the juice of the lime and taste again. Serve up with coriander and chilli slices scattered on top.

CAYENNE-ROASTED SPROUTS WITH CHICKPEAS, APRICOTS & LEMON

I love Brussels sprouts, but not when they're boiled. In my opinion, they need to be eaten raw or sautéed or roasted until very crisp and charred. This recipe does just that, with the welcome addition of some sweetness from the dried apricots, and extra protein in the form of chickpeas, all tied together with a lovely harissa yogurt.

250 g/9 oz. Brussels sprouts	Broccoli, cauliflower, cabbage (cut into wedges)
80 g/½ cup dried apricots	Any dried fruit, but if small, only place in oven for 2–3 minutes
400-g/14-oz. can of chickpeas	Any legume or pea, but avoid butter/lima beans
1 garlic bulb	Essential
½ lemon	Lime or orange
½ teaspoon cayenne pepper	Smoked or sweet paprika, or chilli powder but only ¼ teaspoon
3 tablespoons olive oil	Any oil will work
200 g/scant 1 cup natural yogurt	Any plain yogurt
1 tablespoon harissa	Dukkah spice mix or sriracha sauce
sea salt and freshly ground pepper	
SERVES 4	**TOTAL TIME 35 MINUTES**

Preheat the oven to 200°C fan/220°C/425°F/Gas 7.

Halve the Brussels sprouts and dried apricots, then drain and rinse the chickpeas and separate the garlic bulb (but leave the individual cloves in their skins). Cut the lemon half into wedges. Place the sprouts, chickpeas, garlic cloves, cayenne pepper, olive oil and some seasoning all on a large baking sheet. Squeeze over the lemon wedges, then add the wedges to the baking sheet. Using your hands, fold all of the ingredients into one another, to coat and combine.

Place the baking sheet on the top shelf of the preheated oven and roast for 25 minutes.

Remove the baking sheet from the oven, add the apricot halves and fold through the roasted ingredients, then return to the oven for a final 5 minutes.

While the apricots get warmed up, mix the yogurt and harissa together, with a small drizzle of olive oil and a good pinch of seasoning. Spread the yogurt liberally over a serving dish, then once the roast items are ready and out of the oven, pile them on top of the yogurt and serve.

GOES WELL WITH Anything! Leftover roast meat, or as a side dish for a winter feast.

LEFTOVERS Great in a toastie with mozzarella and cranberry sauce!

LAMB HOT POT

This is one of my most treasured winter meals, always has been, always will be. The best thing about a traditional hot pot is that you don't need to brown the meat, so it is very quick to get in the oven. I've kept this recipe fairly true to the original Lancashire hot pot, but have added some carrot (do add more veg should you want to use it up).

800 g/1 lb. 12 oz. lamb neck fillet	Lamb shoulder or leg
2 large onions	Any colour onion, or leek or more carrot
200 g/7 oz. carrots (about 4 small)	Leeks, celeriac/celery root, swede/rutabaga, whatever veg you want to use up
20 g/2⅓ tablespoons plain/all-purpose flour	Any flour you have
2 bay leaves	Not essential but lovely, or a little rosemary or oregano
3 sprigs of fresh thyme	Not essential but lovely, or a little rosemary or oregano
500 ml/2 cups lamb stock	Use chicken stock
500 g/1 lb. 2 oz. potatoes	Essential
30 g/2 tablespoons butter	A little oil on top of the potatoes
sea salt and freshly ground pepper	
SERVES 4	**TOTAL TIME 3¼ HOURS**

3-litre/quart pie dish or casserole dish/Dutch oven, with a tight-fitting lid

Preheat the oven to 140°C fan/160°C/325°F/Gas 3.

Chop the lamb neck into 5-6-cm/2–2½-inch chunks. Halve, peel and chop the onions into 2-cm/¾-inch wedges and cut the carrot into 6-cm/2½-inch pieces. Add the lamb and veg to a large mixing bowl, along with the flour and a very generous pinch of seasoning. Mix well to coat the ingredients in the seasoned flour. Tip this mixture, along with the herbs, into your dish. Next, pour in the lamb stock.

Very thinly slice the potatoes (no need to peel), no thicker than 3 mm/⅛ inch (use a mandolin if you have one). Lay them on top of the hot pot in a fan style, as you might if you were making a smart dauphinoise potato dish, then dot the butter all over the top. Add another good pinch of seasoning on top and cover with the tight-fitting lid. If you don't have a lid and are using foil, make sure it's sealed well around the edges.

Cook in the preheated oven for 2 hours, then remove the lid or foil, and cook for another hour. If you'd like the potatoes really crispy, place the dish under the grill/broiler for an extra and final 5 minutes at the end. Let sit for 5 minutes, then serve.

GOES WELL WITH Buttered cabbage or minty peas. And a glass of red.

LEFTOVERS Wonderful as they are, or add some stock and turn it into a broth, which you can load up with more veg, some rice or extra flavours, or even turn it into a curry with some fried onions and curry powder, canned tomatoes etc. Delicious.

CELERY WALDORF

This is a really simple salad, inspired by the classic Waldorf. I often have celery lurking in the fridge, having bought it for a specific recipe and then never finished it, so if you're that person too, give this a go. The salad dressing is a great one for all salads, so keep it in mind for any robust, crunchy leaves or raw veg you want to coat with some flavour.

SALAD	
1 head of celery	Ideal, but also try fennel
150 g/1 cup seedless red grapes	Black or green grapes, raisins, sultanas/golden raisins or dried cranberries
50 g/½ cup walnuts	Almonds, hazelnuts or Brazil nuts; a combination is fine too
30 g/¼ cup pumpkin seeds/pepitas	Sunflower seeds; mixed seeds are great too
DRESSING	
2 tablespoons white wine vinegar	Cider, red wine or sherry vinegar, but not balsamic
1 teaspoon honey	Agave, date syrup, brown sugar of any sort
1 tablespoon Dijon mustard	Grainy, English or American
2 tablespoons extra virgin olive oil	Olive oil, rapeseed/canola oil or walnut oil
olive oil, for roasting	
sea salt and freshly ground pepper	
SERVES 4–6 AS A SIDE	*TOTAL TIME 35 MINUTES*

Preheat the oven to 200°C fan/220°C/425°F/Gas 7.

Pull off any celery leaves (leaving them whole) and add to a large salad bowl. Thinly slice the whole celery at an angle. Scatter a third of the sliced celery on a baking sheet, drizzle with oil and a pinch of seasoning and roast on the top shelf of the preheated oven for about 20 minutes, until lightly caramelized and tender. Add the remaining sliced celery to the salad bowl.

While the celery roasts, thinly slice the grapes as best you can (a small serrated knife is best). They don't need to be really thin, but try to cut each grape into 3 or 4 slices.

Add the grapes to the salad bowl, along with all of the dressing ingredients, then toss really well. Whilst I like to avoid extra dishwashing and not use an extra bowl to mix the dressing, this does mean you need to mix the salad and liquids thoroughly so that they combine and emulsify. So, hands in and a minute or two of gently tossing and turning.

When the roasted celery is done, add the walnuts and pumpkin seeds/pepitas to the baking sheet, toss to coat in the existing oils and return to the oven for a final 5 minutes. Once ready, give them a final jiggle then add to the salad bowl and mix to combine everything. You'll have a crunchy but warm, tart yet sweet, gentle but bold salad ready for you, right there.

GOES WELL WITH I really like this salad with chicken thighs, or try it with crackers, salami and cheese for a take on a traditional ploughman's lunch.

LEFTOVERS Brilliant piled into a sandwich or toastie with some ham and cheese, or even better, rare roast beef leftover from your Sunday roast.

MAPLE-ROASTED CELERIAC WITH FETA & PARSLEY

Celeriac/celery root is already a fairly sweet vegetable, but I love what the maple syrup does to the flavour in this recipe, and then it's all the better for the addition of the salty feta. It's wonderfully simple and very satisfying.

1 celeriac/celery root (about 800 g/ 1 lb. 12 oz.)	Essential
4 tablespoons maple syrup	Honey is the best swap, or date syrup or agave
100 g/3½ oz. feta	Mozzarella, goat's cheese or ricotta
5 g/¼ oz. parsley	Any fresh herb, it's just to freshen things up
olive oil, for roasting	
extra virgin olive oil, for serving	
sea salt and freshly ground pepper	
SERVES 4	**TOTAL TIME 1¼ HOURS**

Preheat the oven to 180°C fan/200°C/400°F/Gas 6.

Trim the base of the celeriac/celery root, then thinly slice down the side of the celeriac with your knife in order to peel the skin (rinse, then freeze the peel and add to your next stock). Cut the celeriac into 2–3-cm/¾–1¼-inch thick wedges and place on a large baking sheet (you may need to use 2 sheets).

Drizzle the maple syrup over the celeriac, following by a good drizzle of olive oil and a very generous scattering of seasoning. Toss to coat and then place on the top shelf of the oven. Let the wedges roast for about 1 hour, turning halfway through – they're ready when golden, tender and smelling amazing.

Place them on a serving dish and top with the feta (just crumble it with your hands), then tear the parsley on top too. Give it all a brief and loose toss to lightly fold everything together, then serve with a final drizzle of extra virgin olive oil.

GOES WELL WITH This is just lovely on its own for lunch, or serve it with roasted chicken thighs for a wholesome supper.

LEFTOVERS This is really lovely made into a 'leftovers frittata' or piled into sandwiches with some of my Romesco Sauce (page 145).

PRUNES IN PORT

This recipe comes from my maternal grandmother, Wawa, and although I never got to enjoy it whilst she was alive, it is a real winter favourite now. It's also great with dates, and plenty of other dried fruits. Got an old bag of raisins, cherries or apricots? Add them too. It lasts for ages and goes with many things, but is best served warm and spooned over ice cream. If you don't have port, use another fortified wine, like sherry, vermouth or Madeira.

500 g/1 lb. 2 oz. prunes	Try with dates or any other dried fruit; cherries, apricots etc
2 bay leaves	Dried is fine if you don't have fresh, or just leave out
1 cinnamon stick	½ teaspoon ground cinnamon or mixed spice
3 cloves	A pinch of ground cloves is fine, or again, mixed spice
a pinch of ground mace	¼ teaspoon freshly grated nutmeg, or just leave out
½ orange, cut into wedges	Add a small splash of orange or apple juice
400 ml/1¾ cups port	Vermouth, sherry, Madeira
30 g/2½ tablespoons demerara/ turbinado sugar	Any sugar – preferably soft light brown, but whatever you have
SERVES 4–6	***TOTAL TIME 40 MINUTES***

Add the prunes, bay leaves, all the spices and orange wedges to a small-medium saucepan and cover with the port. Bring the mixture to the boil, then reduce the heat to a very gentle simmer and let bubble for 30 minutes.

After 30 minutes, add the sugar and gently stir to get it all mixed in. Let it gently bubble for another 5 minutes, until the liquid thickens up and you have a loose, syrupy consistency.

Wawa would say that if the prunes become too soft, scoop them out of the pan while you continue to reduce the liquid, then stir them through at the end.

GOES WELL WITH Ice cream!

LEFTOVERS Continue to serve with ice cream or yogurt, or add to a cheese board. And I plan to try folding strained prunes into a cake batter – surely that would be amazing?

CITRUS JELLIES

I love jelly – it reminds me of childhood, and I don't understand anyone who doesn't enjoy jelly served with ice cream or cream. This recipe uses whatever citrus fruits you have – lemons, limes, oranges, grapefruits, pomelo, blood oranges, tangerines, clementines. Make one individual flavour, or mix them up, I promise the jellies will be delicious in whatever combination you conjure up.

5 gelatine leaves	You need the gelatine for this recipe
100 ml/7 tablespoons citrus fruit juice (2 oranges provide roughly this quantity), plus zest	Any citrus fruit – I particularly like using blood oranges when they're in season
120 g/⅔ cup minus 1 tablespoon caster/superfine sugar	You need the caster sugar, but you could use golden or granulated
400 ml/1¾ cups water	
SERVES 6–8	*TOTAL TIME 30 MINUTES, PLUS SETTING*

4–6 small glass tumblers to set and serve the jelly in

Add the gelatine leaves to a bowl filled with cold water. Set aside to soak.

Zest the citrus fruits, then juice them. Next, add the sugar, water and citrus juice and zest to a saucepan and slowly bring to just under a boil – this should be done gently and take about 10 minutes as you want all of the sugar to dissolve.

Pour the mixture into a measuring jug/pitcher, through a sieve/strainer to collect any bits, then let it cool a little in the jug for 5 minutes. Squeeze out the now supple gelatine leaves, using your hands to get rid of any excess water, then add them to the citrus liquid in the measuring jug. Stir very well to fully dissolve the gelatine, then pour into your serving glasses.

Let the jellies cool down, then place in the fridge and leave to set overnight.

GOES WELL WITH Anything creamy... ice cream, single/light cream, double/heavy cream, clotted cream...

LEFTOVERS They'll last in the fridge for a good few days, so just save them for evening treats.

INDEX

THANK YOUS

Well, the fact that I'm writing this means *Fridge Raid* is almost in the hands of readers at home! This book really feels like a bit of a blur, but in a good way. Worldwide pandemic, a high-risk pregnancy, then writing, testing, developing and food styling a book, all locked up in our London home. Just me, Hal my husband, our two cats (and a growing bump) – it was quite the experience. The success of which, I'll include the bump in that, wouldn't have been possible without so many people supporting me and making things as smooth and enjoyable as possible, so here goes.

To the RPS team, firstly Cindy Richards and Julia Charles for continuing to believe in me and facilitating the creation of *Fridge Raid*! The process has been positive throughout and I've felt nothing other than respected and free to do 'my thing'; I've been able to turn my vision into reality (collectively, of course) without creative restriction or manipulation. I'm also particularly grateful for you allowing the 'as comfortable as possible' shoot set-up, mid first trimester stress and strain, which was such a relief and really easy – thank you so much.

To Gillian Haslam, for being the most lovely, relaxed, encouraging and supportive editor; it was a solidly virtual editor/author relationship and so I'm hoping by the time I see this in print we have been allowed to meet... and dare I wish it... hug!?

To Leslie Harrington and particularly Megan Smith, for art directing and designing another beautiful, honest, refreshing and colourful book with tones and palettes I can't help but swoon over. Megs, you get my style and attitude towards food clearly and have been so instrumental in getting that down on paper, bringing everything to life so wonderfully. I love what you've done with the design, thank you, you're a dream.

To the marketing and sales teams, Yvonne Doolan in particular, thank you for all your work spreading the word and keeping me updated and involved. This is a huge bulk of work, but one that mainly happens a bit later on, so thank you in advance for all your efforts.

To the very special shoot team of Rita Platts, Hannah Wilkinson and Sarah Vassallo – what a treat it was. The photo shoot was the first proper stint of social interaction we had all had for quite a while, albeit masked and sanitized up, but still, it was such a special ten days hanging out and working with you.

Rita, I love your work and how you've captured the recipes and little snippets of *Fridge Raid* life, you're so talented and a complete ray of sunshine. Even better, we've realized we live about 300 metres from each other, so I've not only gained a new friend, but a very lovely set of neighbours in your family.

Hannah, your props styling has been just brilliant and whilst it was sad you couldn't be on set because of lockdown restrictions, it was so exciting opening up the props deliveries and seeing what you'd carefully and perfectly selected. You also put extra work into making your absence as simple as possible, with your communication and extra documents to help us allocate everything, thank you for that – it really was so useful and diligent of you.

Sarah, what an ally you are. You were the most efficient, organized and sweet partner to me in the kitchen. Thank you for assisting me on the shoot and being so generous with your work ethic, attitude and simply lovely personality. I'm also extra grateful for all the lugging around of backgrounds and boxes that you and Rita took on whilst I couldn't. I already miss our mornings of tea and toast pre-shoot, along with the rare, but cherished, garden lunches in the sunshine. It really didn't feel like work most of the time.

I must say a big thank you to my home testers, who gallantly received emails laden with recipes and cooked away at home, sending notes and feedback, which is always so very helpful. It can be a fairly solitary and consuming process writing a whole book's worth of recipes alone, so getting a plethora of outside eyes, and taste buds, is invaluable. Thank you to Summer, Angie, Peter, Vivien, Harriet, Bryn, Anna, Samson, Becky, Gus, Meg, Bryony, Nicky, Ros, Lotty, Beilby, Hermione, Fi, Izzy, Julia, Katy, Ben and Wills.

Finally, to my Hal, for being yet again the most obedient tester and washer-upper throughout the writing and testing process. Writing a cookbook whilst battling morning sickness, fatigue, cramps, headaches and anxiety was not quite the convenient timing I'd naively assumed... and it was you who made it all manageable and somehow enjoyable, even when I felt my worst. Thank you for being the ultimate husband, best friend, polite critic... and always impressive eater.